HEALTH
FROM
GREAT

HEALTH SECRETS
FROM THE
GREAT GURUS

JOSEPH MURPHY
DALE CARNEGIE
WILLIAM W ATKINSON
WALLACE D WATTLES

An imprint of
Srishti Publishers & Distributors

Srishti Publishers & Distributors
A unit of AJR Publishing LLP
212A, Peacock Lane
Shahpur Jat, New Delhi – 110 049
editorial@srishtipublishers.com

First published by Bold,
an imprint of Srishti Publishers & Distributors in 2022

Printed and bound in India

CONTENTS

Contents

MEMORY: HOW TO DEVELOP, TRAIN AND USE IT
William Walker Atkinson

THE SCIENCE OF BEING WELL
Wallace D Wattles

THE KEY TO READING THIS BOOK

The idea behind this book germinated from the concern faced by millions of people across the world – health. It reads like a small word, but the impact it has on all of us is immense.

With rising expectations in everyday life, and great goals to be achieved, it has become essential to fortify one's health first. After all, a strong foundation of healthy lifestyle ensures a positive outcome in all spheres of life!

This book focuses on overall development of your personality, encapsulating within its pages effective ways to enrich your lives – physically, mentally, emotionally and spiritually.

The core message of the book remains that the vital energy for achieving anything in life rests within us. We possess all that is needed to attain success; we just need to awaken it and start using these principles in everyday life.

A compilation of valuable knowledge from four great works, *Health Secrets from the Great Gurus* is a book that will change your life. You will find in these pages the secret to good health, happiness, mental peace and emotional balance.

The Power of Your Subconscious Mind is a masterpiece by Dr Joseph Murphy, who has put down in words his experience of years. The book reflects the power that our mind holds and how best we can channelize it for self-growth and improvement.

Dale Carnegie is well known across the globe for his unmatched wisdom and insights on shaping personalities. In the sections from *How to Stop Worrying and Start Living*, you can learn how to reduce your worries, and adopt a growth-oriented lifestyle.

Memory by William Walker Atkinson is a tool to sharpen your skill at remembering and recollecting things quickly. With actionable tips on how to remember dates, names, people, places, events, etc., this is a commendable read.

The Science of Being Well is Wallace D Wattles' popular book on basic aspects in everyday life that define our health and overall well-being. With smart tips on managing sleep, breathing and eating habits, it can be instrumental in attaining good health.

As you dive into the book, we advise you to put into action whatever you read in these pages – slowly, but steadily. Sincere effort combined with these ideas is bound to get you exceptional results.

THE POWER OF
YOUR SUBCONSCIOUS MIND

Joseph Murphy

1

THE TREASURE HOUSE
WITHIN YOU

Infinite riches are all around you if you will open your mental eyes and behold the treasure house of infinity within you. There is a gold mine within you from which you can extract everything you need to live life gloriously, joyously, and abundantly.

Many are sound asleep because they do not know about this gold mine of infinite intelligence and boundless love within themselves. Whatever you want, you can draw forth. A magnetized piece of steel will lift about twelve times its own weight, and if you demagnetize this same piece of steel, it will not even lift a feather. Similarly, there are two types of men. There is the magnetized man who is full of confidence and faith. He knows that he is born to win and to succeed. Then, there is the type of man who is demagnetized. He is full of fears and doubts. Opportunities come, and he says, "I might fail; I might lose my money; people will laugh at me." This type of man will not get very far in life because, if he is afraid to go forward, he will simply stay where he is. Become a magnetized man and discover the master secret of the ages.

The master secret of the ages

What, in your opinion, is the master secret of the ages? The secret of atomic energy? Thermonuclear energy? The neutron bomb? Interplanetary travel? No – not any of these. Then, what is this master secret? Where can one find it, and how can it be contacted and brought into action? The answer is extraordinarily simple. This secret is the marvellous, miracle-working power found in your own subconscious mind, the last place that most people would seek it.

The marvellous power of your subconscious

You can bring into your life more power, more wealth, more health, more happiness, and more joy by learning to contact and release the hidden power of your subconscious mind.

You need not acquire this power; you already possess it. But, you want to learn how to use it; you want to understand it so that you can apply it in all departments of your life.

As you follow the simple techniques and processes set forth in this book, you can gain the necessary knowledge and under-standing. A new light can inspire you, and you can generate a new force enabling you to realize your hopes and make all your dreams come true. Decide now to make your life grander, greater, richer, and nobler than ever before.

Within your subconscious depths lie infinite wisdom, infinite power, and infinite supply of all that is necessary, which is waiting for development and expression. Begin now to recognize these potentialities of your deeper mind, and they will take form in the world without.

The infinite intelligence within your subconscious mind can reveal to you everything you need to know at every moment of time and point of space, provided you are open-minded and receptive. You can receive new thoughts and ideas, enabling you to bring forth new inventions, make new discoveries, or write books and plays. Moreover, the infinite intelligence in your sub-conscious can impart to you wonderful kinds of knowledge of an original nature. It can reveal to you and open the way for perfect expression and true place in your life.

Through the wisdom of your subconscious mind you can attract the ideal companion, as well as the right business associate or partner. It can find the right buyer for your home, and provide you with all the money you need, and the financial freedom to be, to do, and to go, as your heart desires.

It is your right to discover this inner world of thought, feeling, and power; of light, love, and beauty. Though invisible, its forces are mighty. Within your subconscious mind you will find the solution for every problem, and the cause for every effect. Because you can draw out the hidden powers, you come into actual possession of the power and wisdom necessary to move forward in abundance, security, joy, and dominion.

I have seen the power of the subconscious lift people up out of crippled states, making them whole, vital, and strong once more, and free to go out into the world to experience happiness, health, and joyous expression. There is a miraculous healing power in your subconscious that can heal the troubled mind and the broken heart. It can open the prison door of the mind and liberate you. It can free you from all kinds of material and physical bondage.

Necessity of a working basis

Substantial progress in any field of endeavour is impossible in the absence of a working basis, which is universal in its application. You can become skilled in the operation of your subconscious mind. You can practice its powers with a certainty of results in exact proportion to your knowledge of its principles and to your application of them for definite specific purposes and goals you wish to achieve.

If you combine hydrogen and oxygen in the proportions of two atoms of the former to one of the latter, water would be the result. You are very familiar with the fact that one atom of oxygen and one atom of carbon will produce carbon monoxide, a poisonous gas. But, if you add another atom of oxygen, you will get carbon dioxide, a harmless gas, and so on throughout the vast realm of chemical compounds.

You must not think that the principles of chemistry, physics, and mathematics differ from the principles of your subconscious mind. Let us consider a generally accepted principle: "Water seeks its own level." This is a universal principle, which is applicable to water everywhere.

Consider another principle: "Matter expands when heated." This is true anywhere, at any time, and under all circumstances. You can heat a piece of steel, and it will expand regardless whether the steel is found in China, England, or India. It is a universal truth that matter expands when heated. It is also a universal truth that whatever you impress on your subconscious mind is expressed on the screen of space as condition, experience, and event.

Your prayer is answered because your subconscious mind is principle, and by principle I mean the way a thing works. For example, the principle of electricity is that it works from a higher to a lower potential. You do not change the principle of electricity when you use it, but by co-operating with nature, you can bring forth marvellous inventions and discoveries, which bless humanity in countless ways.

Your subconscious mind is principle and works according to the law of belief. You must know what belief is, why it works, and how it works.

The law of your mind is the law of belief. This means to believe in the way your mind works, to believe in belief itself. The belief of your mind is the thought of your mind – that is simple – just that and nothing else.

All your experiences, events, conditions, and acts are the reactions of your subconscious mind to your thoughts. Remember, it is not the thing believed in, but the belief in your own mind, which brings about the result.

Cease believing in the false beliefs, opinions, superstitions, and fears of mankind. Begin to believe in the eternal verities and truths of life, which never change. Then, you will move onward, upward, and god-ward.

Whoever reads this book and applies the principles of the subconscious mind herein set forth; will be able to pray scientifically and effectively for himself and for others. Your prayer is answered according to the universal law of action and reaction. Thought is incipient action. The reaction is the response from your subconscious mind which corresponds with the nature of your thought. Busy your mind with the concepts of harmony, health, peace, and good will, and wonders will happen in your life.

The duality of mind

You have only one mind, but your mind possesses two distinctive characteristics. The line of demarcation between the two is well known to all thinking men and women today. The two functions of your mind are essentially unlike. Each is endowed with separate and distinct attributes and powers. The nomenclature generally used to distinguish the two functions of your mind is as follows: The objective and subjective mind, the conscious and subconscious mind, the waking and sleeping mind, the surface self and the deep self, the voluntary mind and the involuntary mind, the male and the female, and many other terms. You will find the terms "conscious" and "subconscious" used to represent the dual nature of your mind throughout this book.

The conscious and subconscious minds

An excellent way to get acquainted with the two functions of your mind is to look upon your own mind as a garden. You are a gardener, and you are planting seeds (thoughts) in your subconscious mind all day long, based on your habitual thinking. As you sow in your subconscious mind, so shall you reap in your body and environment.

Begin now to sow thoughts of peace, happiness, right action, good will, and prosperity. Think quietly and with interest on these qualities and accept them fully in your conscious reasoning mind. Continue to plant these wonderful seeds (thoughts) in the garden of your mind, and you will reap a glorious harvest. Your subconscious mind may be likened to the soil, which will grow all kinds of seeds, good or bad.

Do men gather grapes of thorns, or figs of thistles? Every thought is, therefore, a cause, and every condition is an effect. For this reason, it is essential that you take charge of your thoughts so as to bring forth only desirable conditions. When your mind thinks correctly, when you understand the truth, when the thoughts deposited in your subconscious mind are constructive, harmonious, and peaceful, and the magic working power of your subconscious will respond and bring about harmonious conditions, agreeable surroundings, and the best of everything. When you begin to control your thought processes, you can apply the powers of your subconscious to any problem or difficulty. In other words, you will actually be consciously cooperating with the infinite power and omnipotent law, which governs all things.

Look around you wherever you live and you will notice that the vast majority of mankind lives in the world without, but the more enlightened men are intensely interested in the world within. Remember, it is the world within, namely, your thoughts, feelings, and imagery that makes your world without. It is, therefore, the only creative power, and everything, which you find in your world of expression, has been created by you in the inner world of your mind consciously or unconsciously.

Knowledge of the interaction of your conscious and subconscious minds will enable you to transform your whole life. In order to change external conditions, you must change the cause. Most men try to change conditions and circumstances by working with conditions and circumstances. To remove discord, confusion, lack, and limitation, you must remove the cause, and the cause is the way you are using your conscious mind. In other words, the way you are thinking and picturing in your mind.

You are living in a fathomless sea of infinite riches. Your subconscious is very sensitive to your thoughts. Your thoughts form the mould or matrix through which the infinite intelligence, wisdom, vital forces, and energies of your subconscious flow. The

practical application of the laws of your mind as illustrated in ea
chapter of this book will cause you to experience abundance for
poverty, wisdom for superstition and ignorance, peace for pain,
joy for sadness, light for darkness, harmony for discord, faith and
confidence for fear, success for failure, and freedom from the law of
averages. Certainly, there can be no more wonderful blessing than
these from a mental, emotional, and material standpoint. Most of
the great scientists, artists, poets, singers, writers, and inventors
have a deep understanding of the workings of the conscious and
subconscious minds.

One time Caruso, the great operatic tenor, was struck with
stage fright. He said his throat was paralyzed due to spasms
caused by intense fear, which constricted the muscles of his throat.
Perspiration poured copiously down his face. He was ashamed
because in a few minutes he had to go out on the stage, yet he was
shaking with fear and trepidation. He said, "They will laugh at me.
I can't sing." Then he shouted in the presence of those behind the
stage, "The Little Me wants to strangle the Big Me within."

He said to the Little Me, "Get out of here, the Big Me wants to
sing through me." By the Big Me, he meant the limitless power and
wisdom of his subconscious mind, and he began to shout, "Get
out, get out, the Big Me is going to sing!"

His subconscious mind responded releasing the vital forces
within him.

When the call came, he walked out on the stage and sang
gloriously and majestically, enthralling the audience.

you now that Caruso must have understood
nd – the conscious or rational, and the sub-
irrational level. Your subconscious mind is reactive
and responds to the nature of your thoughts. When your conscious
mind (the Little Me) is full of fear, worry, and anxiety, the negative
emotions engendered in your subconscious mind (the Big Me)
are released and flood the conscious mind with a sense of panic,
foreboding, and despair. When this happens, you can, like Caruso,
speak affirmatively and with a deep sense of authority to the
irrational emotions generated in your deeper mind as follows: "Be
still, be quiet, I am in control, you must obey me, you are subject
to my command, you cannot intrude where you do not belong."

It is fascinating and intensely interesting to observe how you
can speak authoritatively and with conviction to the irrational
movement of your deeper self bringing silence, harmony, and
peace to your mind. The subconscious is subject to the conscious
mind, and that is why it is called subconscious or subjective.

Outstanding differences and modes of operation

You will perceive the main differences by the following illustrations
– The conscious mind is like the navigator or captain at the bridge
of a ship. He directs the ship and signals orders to men in the engine
room, who in turn control all the boilers, instruments, gauges, etc.
The men in the engine room do not know where they are going;
they follow orders. They would go on the rocks if the man on the
bridge issued faulty or wrong instructions based on his findings

with the compass, sextant, or other instruments. The men in the engine room obey him because he is in charge and issues orders, which are automatically obeyed. Members of the crew do not talk back to the captain; they simply carry out orders.

The captain is the master of his ship, and his decrees are carried out. Likewise, your conscious mind is the captain and the master of your ship, which represents your body, environment and all your affairs. Your subconscious mind takes the orders you give it based upon what your conscious mind believes and accepts as true.

When you repeatedly say to people, "I can't afford it," then your subconscious mind takes you at your word and sees to it that you will not be in a position to purchase what you want. As long as you persist in saying, "I can't afford that car, that trip to Europe, that home" you can rest assured that your subconscious mind will follow your orders, and you will go through life experiencing the lack of all these things.

Last Christmas Eve a beautiful young university student looked at an attractive and rather expensive traveling bag in a store window. She was going home to Buffalo, New York, for the holidays. She was about to say, "I can't afford that bag," when she recalled something she had heard at one of my lectures which was, "Never finish a negative statement; reverse it immediately, and wonders will happen in your life."

She said, "That bag is mine. It is for sale. I accept it mentally, and my subconscious sees to it that I receive it."

At eight o'clock Christmas Eve her fiancé presented her with a bag exactly the same as the one she had looked at and mentally identified herself with at ten o'clock the same morning. She had filled her mind with the thought of expectancy and released the whole thing to her deeper mind, which has the "know-how" of accomplishment.

This young girl, a student at the University of Southern California, said to me, "I didn't have the money to buy that bag, but now I know where to find money and all the things I need, and that is in the treasure house of eternity within me."

Another simple illustration is this: When you say, "I do not like mushrooms," and the occasion subsequently comes that you are served mushrooms in sauces or salads, you will get indigestion because your subconscious mind says to you, "The boss (your conscious mind) does not like mushrooms." This is an amusing example of the outstanding differences and modes of operation of your conscious and subconscious minds.

A woman may say, "I wake up at three o'clock, if I drink coffee at night." Whenever she drinks coffee, her subconscious mind nudges her, as if to say, "The boss wants you to stay awake tonight."

Your subconscious mind works twenty-four hours a day and makes provisions for your benefit, pouring all the fruit of your habitual thinking into your lap.

How her subconscious responded

A woman wrote to me a few months ago as follows: "I am seventy-five years old, a widow with a grown family. I was living alone and on a pension. I heard your lectures on the powers of the subconscious mind wherein you said that ideas could be conveyed to the subconscious mind by repetition, faith, and expectancy.

"I began to repeat frequently with feeling, 'I am wanted. I am happily married to a kind, loving, and spiritual-minded man. I am secure!'

"I kept on doing this many times a day for about two weeks, and one day at the corner drugstore, I was introduced to a retired pharmacist. I found him to be kind, understanding, and very religious. He was a perfect answer to my prayer. Within a week he proposed to me, and now we are on our honeymoon in Europe. I know that the intelligence within my subconscious mind brought both of us together in divine order."

This woman discovered that the treasure house was within her. Her prayer was felt as true in her heart, and her affirmation sank down by osmosis into her subconscious mind, which is the creative medium. The moment she succeeded in bringing about a subjective embodiment, her subconscious mind brought about the answer through the law of attraction.

Her deeper mind, full of wisdom and intelligence, brought both of them together in divine order.

Be sure that you think on *whatsoever things are true, whatsoever things are honest, whatsoever things are just, whatsoever things are pure, whatsoever things are lovely, whatsoever things are of good report; if there be any virtue, and if there be any praise, think on these things.*

Brief summary of ideas worth remembering

The treasure house is within you. Look within for the answer to your heart's desire.

The great secret possessed by the great men of all ages was their ability to contact and release the powers of their subconscious mind. You can do the same.

Your subconscious has the answer to all problems. If you suggest to your subconscious prior to sleep, "I want to get up at 6 a.m.," it will awaken you at that exact time.

Your subconscious mind is the builder of your body and can heal you. Lull yourself to sleep every night with the idea of perfect health, and your subconscious, being your faithful servant, will obey you.

Every thought is a cause, and every condition is an effect.

If you want to write a book, write a wonderful play, give a better talk to your audience, convey the idea lovingly and feelingly to your subconscious mind, and it will respond accordingly.

You are like a captain navigating a ship. He must give the right orders, and likewise, you must give the right orders (thoughts and images) to your subconscious mind, which controls and governs all your experiences.

Never use the terms, "I can't afford it" or "I can't do this." Your subconscious mind takes you at your word and sees to it that you do not have the money or the ability to do what you want to do. Affirm, "I can do all things through the power of my subconscious mind."

The law of life is the law of belief. A belief is a thought in your mind. Do not believe in things to harm or hurt you. Believe in the power of your subconscious to heal, inspire, strengthen, and prosper you. According to your belief is it done unto you.

Change your thoughts, and you change your destiny.

2

MENTAL HEALINGS
IN MODERN TIMES

Everyone is definitely concerned with the healing of bodily conditions and human affairs. What is it that heals? Where is this healing power? These are questions asked by everyone. The answer is that this healing power is stored in the subconscious mind of each person, and a changed mental attitude on the part of the sick person releases this healing power.

No mental or religious science practitioner, psychologist, psychiatrist, or medical doctor ever healed a patient. There is an old saying, "The doctor dresses the wound, but god heals it." The psychologist or psychiatrist proceeds to remove the mental blocks in the patient so that the healing principle may be released, restoring the patient to health. Likewise, the surgeon removes the physical block enabling the healing currents to function normally.

No physician, surgeon, or mental science practitioner claims, "He healed the patient." The one healing power is called by many names – Nature, Life, God, Creative Intelligence, and Subconscious Power.

As previously outlined, there are many different methods used to remove the mental, emotional, and physical blocks which inhibit the flow of the healing life animating all of us. The healing principle resident in your subconscious mind can and will, if properly directed by you or some other person, heal your mind and body of all disease. This healing principle is operative in all men regardless of creed, colour, or race. You do not have to belong to some particular church in order to use and participate in this healing process. Your subconscious will heal the burn or cut on your hand even though you profess to be an atheist or agnostic.

The modern mental therapeutic procedure is based on the truth that the infinite intelligence and power of your subconscious mind responds according to your faith. The mental science practitioner or minister follows the injunction of the Bible, i.e., he goes into his closet and shuts the door, which means he stills his mind, relaxes, lets go, and thinks of the infinite healing presence within him. He closes the door of his mind to all outside distractions as well as appearances, and then he quietly and knowingly turns over his request or desire to his subconscious mind, realizing that the intelligence of his mind will answer him according to his specific needs.

17

The most wonderful thing to know is this: Imagine the end desired and feel its reality; then the infinite life principle will respond to your conscious choice and your conscious request. This is the meaning of *believe you have received, and you shall receive.* This is what the modern mental scientist does when he practices prayer therapy.

One process of healing

There is only one universal healing principle operating through everything – the cat, the dog, the tree, the grass, the wind, the earth – for everything is alive. This life principle operates through the animal, vegetable, and mineral kingdoms as instinct and the law of growth. Man is consciously aware of this life principle, and he can consciously direct it to bless himself in countless ways. There are many different approaches, techniques, and methods in using the universal power, but there is only one process of healing, which is faith, for *according to your faith is it done unto you.*

The law of belief

All religions of the world represent forms of belief, and these beliefs are explained in many ways. The law of life is belief. What do you believe about yourself, life, and the universe? *It is done unto you, as you believe.*

Belief is a thought in your mind, which causes the power of your subconscious to be distributed into all phases of your life according to your thinking habits. You must realize that we are not talking about your belief in some ritual, ceremony, form, institution, man, or formula. It is talking about belief itself. The belief of your mind is simply the thought of your mind. Everything is possible for those who believe.

It is foolish to believe in something to hurt or harm you. Remember, it is not the thing believed in that hurts or harms you, but the belief or thought in your mind, which creates the result. All your experiences, all your actions, and all the events and circumstances of your life are but the reflections and reactions to your own thought.

Prayer therapy is the combined function of the conscious and subconscious mind scientifically directed

Prayer therapy is the synchronized, harmonious, and intelligent function of the conscious and subconscious levels of mind specifically directed for a definite purpose. In scientific prayer or prayer therapy, you must know what you are doing and why you are doing it. You trust the law of healing. Prayer therapy is sometimes referred to as mental treatment, and another term is scientific prayer.

In prayer therapy you consciously choose a certain idea, mental picture, or plan which you desire to experience. You realize your capacity to convey this idea or mental image to your subconscious by feeling the reality of the state assumed. As you remain faithful in your mental attitude, your prayer will be answered. Prayer therapy is a definite mental action for a definite specific purpose.

Let us suppose that you decide to heal a certain difficulty by prayer therapy. You are aware that your problem or sickness, whatever it may be, must be caused by negative thoughts charged with fear and lodged in your subconscious mind, and that if you can succeed in cleansing your mind of these thoughts, you will get a healing.

You, therefore, turn to the healing power within your own subconscious mind and remind yourself of its infinite power and intelligence and its capacity to heal all conditions. As you dwell on these truths, your fear will begin to dissolve, and the recollection of these truths also corrects the erroneous beliefs.

You give thanks for the healing that you know will come, and then you keep your mind off the difficulty until you feel guided, after an interval, to pray again. While you are praying, you absolutely refuse to give any power to the negative conditions or to admit for a second that the healing will not come. This attitude of mind brings about the harmonious union of the conscious and subconscious mind, which releases the healing power.

Faith healing, what it means, and how blind faith works

What is popularly termed faith healing is not the faith mentioned in scriptures, which means knowledge of the interaction of the conscious and subconscious mind. A faith healer is one who heals without any real scientific understanding of the powers and forces involved. He may claim that he has a special gift of healing, and the sick person's blind belief in him or his powers may bring results.

The voodoo doctor in South Africa and other parts of the world may heal by incantations, or touching the so-called bones of saints, or anything else may heal a person, which cause the patients to honestly believe in the method or process.

Any method, which causes you to move from fear and worry to faith and expectancy, will heal. There are many persons, each of whom claims that because his personal theory produces results, it is, therefore, the correct one. This, as already explained in this chapter, cannot be true.

To illustrate how blind faith works: You will recall our discussion of the Swiss physician, Franz Anton Mesmer. In 1776 he claimed many cures when he stroked diseased bodies with artificial magnets. Later on he threw away his magnets and evolved the theory of animal magnetism. This he held to be a fluid, which pervades the universe, but is most active in the human organism.

He claimed that this magnetic fluid, which was going forth from him to his patients, healed them. People flocked to him, and many wonderful cures were affected. Mesmer moved to Paris, and while there the Government appointed a commission composed of physicians and members of the Academy of Science, of which Benjamin Franklin was a member, to investigate his cures.

The report admitted the leading facts claimed by Mesmer, but held that there was no evidence to prove the correctness of his magnetic fluid theory, and said the effects were due to the imagination of the patients.

Soon after this, Mesmer was driven into exile, and died in 1815. Shortly afterwards, Dr. Braid of Manchester undertook to show that magnetic fluid had nothing to do with the production of the healings of Dr. Mesmer. Dr. Braid discovered that patients could be thrown into hypnotic sleep by suggestion; during which many of the well-known phenomena ascribed to magnetism by Mesmer could be produced.

You can readily see that all these cures were undoubtedly brought about by the active imagination of the patients together with a powerful suggestion of health to their subconscious minds. All this could be termed blind faith, as there was no understanding in those days as to how the cures were brought about.

Summary of your aids to health

Find out what it is that heals you. Realize that correct directions given to your subconscious mind will heal your mind and body.

Develop a definite plan for turning over your requests or desires to your subconscious mind.

Imagine the end desired and feel its reality. Follow it through, and you will get definite results.

Decide what belief is. Know that belief is a thought in your mind, and what you think you create.

It is foolish to believe in sickness and something to hurt or to harm you. Believe in perfect health, prosperity, peace, wealth, and divine guidance.

Great and noble thoughts upon which you habitually dwell become great acts.

Apply the power of prayer therapy in your life. Choose a certain plan, idea, or mental picture. Mentally and emotionally unite with that idea, and as you remain faithful to your mental attitude, your prayer will be answered.

Always remember, if you really want the power to heal, you can have it through faith, which means knowledge of the working of your conscious and subconscious mind. Faith comes with understanding. Blind faith means that a person may get results in healing without any scientific understanding of the powers and forces involved.

Learn to pray for your loved ones who may be ill. Quiet your mind, and your thoughts of health, vitality, and perfection operating through the one universal subjective mind will be felt and resurrected in the mind of your loved one.

3

PRACTICAL TECHNIQUES
IN MENTAL HEALINGS

An engineer has a technique and a process for building a bridge or an engine. Like the engineer, your mind also has a technique for governing, controlling, and directing your life. You must realize that methods and techniques are primary.

In building the Golden Gate Bridge, the chief engineer understood mathematical principles, stresses and strains. Secondly, he had a picture of the ideal bridge across the bay. The third step was his application of tried and proven methods by which the principles were implemented until the bridge took form and we drive on it. There also are techniques and methods by which your prayers are answered. If your prayer is answered, there is a way in which it is answered, and this is a scientific way. Nothing happens by chance. This is a world of law and order. In this chapter you will find practical techniques for the unfolding and nurturing of your spiritual life. Your prayers must not remain up in the air like a balloon. They must go somewhere and accomplish something in your life.

When we come to analyze prayer we discover there are many different approaches and methods. We will not consider in this book the formal, ritual prayers used in religious services. These have an important place in group worship. We are immediately concerned with the methods of personal prayer as it is applied in your daily life and as it is used to help others.

Prayer is the formulation of an idea concerning something we wish to accomplish. Prayer is the soul's sincere desire. Your desire is your prayer. It comes out of your deepest needs and it reveals the things you want in life. *Blessed are they that hunger and thirst after righteousness: for they shall be filled.* That is really prayer, life's hunger and thirst for peace, harmony, health, joy, and all the other blessings of life.

The passing-over technique for impregnating the subconscious

This consists essentially in inducing the subconscious mind to take over your request as handed it by the conscious mind. This passing over is best accomplished in the reverie-like state. Know that in your deeper mind are Infinite Intelligence and Infinite Power. Just calmly think over what you want; see it coming into fuller fruition from this moment forward. Be like the little girl who had a very bad cough and a sore throat. She declared firmly and repeatedly, "It is passing away now. It is passing away now." It passed away in about an hour. Use this technique with complete simplicity and naïveté.

Your subconscious will accept your blueprint

If you were building a new home for yourself and family, you know that you would be intensely interested in regard to the blueprint for your home; you would see to it that the builders conformed to the blueprint. You would watch the material and select only the best wood, steel, in fact, the best of everything. What about your mental home and your mental blueprint for happiness and abundance? All your experiences and everything that enters into your life depend upon the nature of the mental building blocks, which you use in the construction of your mental home.

If your blueprint is full of mental patterns of fear, worry, anxiety, or lack, and if you are despondent, doubtful, and cynical, then the texture of the mental material you are weaving into your mind will come forth as more toil, care, tension, anxiety, and limitation of all kinds.

The most fundamental and the most far-reaching activity in life is that which you build into your mentality every waking hour. Your word is silent and invisible; nevertheless, it is real.

You are building your mental home all the time, and your thought and mental imagery represent your blueprint. Hour by hour, moment by moment, you can build radiant health, success, and happiness by the thoughts you think, the ideas which you harbor, the beliefs that you accept, and the scenes that you rehearse in the hidden studio of your mind. This stately mansion, upon the construction of which you are perpetually engaged, is your personality, your identity in this plane, your whole life story on this earth.

Get a new blueprint; build silently by realizing peace, harmony, joy, and good will in the present moment. By dwelling upon these things and claiming them, your subconscious will accept your blueprint and bring all these things to pass. *By their fruits ye shall know them.*

The science and art of true prayer

The term "science" means knowledge, which is coordinated, arranged, and systematized. Let us think of the science and art of true prayer as it deals with the fundamental principles of life and the techniques and processes by which they can be demonstrated in your life, as well as in the life of every human being when he applies them faithfully. The art is your technique or process, and the science behind it is the definite response of creative mind to your mental picture or thought.

Your prayer, which is your mental act must be accepted as an image in your mind before the power from your subconscious will play upon it and make it productive. You must reach a point of acceptance in your mind, an unqualified and undisputed state of agreement.

This contemplation should be accompanied by a feeling of joy and restfulness in foreseeing the certain accomplishment of your desire. The sound basis for the art and science of true prayer is your knowledge and complete confidence that the movement of your conscious mind will gain a definite response from your subconscious mind, which is one with boundless wisdom and infinite power. By following this procedure, your prayers will be answered.

The visualization technique

The easiest and most obvious way to formulate an idea is to visualize it, to see it in your mind's eye as vividly as if it were alive. You can see with the naked eye only what already exists in the external world; in a similar way, that which you can visualize in your mind's eye already exists in the invisible realms of your mind. Any picture, which you have in your mind, is *the substance of things hoped for and the evidence of things not seen.* What you form in your imagination is as real as any part of your body. The idea and the thought are real and will one day appear in your objective world if you are faithful to your mental image.

This process of thinking forms impressions in your mind; these impressions in turn become manifested as facts and experiences in your life.

The builder visualizes the type of building he wants; he sees it as he desires it to be completed. His imagery and thought-processes become a plastic mould from which the building will emerge –

a beautiful or an ugly one, a skyscraper or a very low one. His mental imagery is projected as it is drawn on paper. Eventually, the contractor and his workers gather the essential materials, and the building progresses until it stands finished, conforming perfectly to the mental patterns of the architect.

I use the visualization technique prior to speaking from the platform. I quiet the wheels of my mind in order that I may present to the subconscious mind my images of thought. Then, I picture the entire auditorium and the seats filled with men and women, and each one of them illumined and inspired by the infinite healing presence within each one. I see them as radiant, happy, and free.

Having first built up the idea in my imagination, I quietly sustain it there as a mental picture while I imagine I hear men and women saying, "I am healed," "I feel wonderful," "I've had an instantaneous healing," "I'm transformed." I keep this up for about ten minutes or more, knowing and feeling that each person's mind and body are saturated with love, wholeness, beauty, and perfection. My awareness grows to the point where in my mind I can actually hear the voices of the multitude proclaiming their health and happiness; then I release the whole picture and go onto the platform. Almost every Sunday some people stop and say that their prayers were answered.

Mental movie method

The Chinese say, "A picture is worth a thousand words." William James, the father of American psychology, stressed the fact that the subconscious mind will bring to pass any picture held in the mind and backed by faith. *Act as though I am, and I will be.*

A number of years ago I was in the Middle West lecturing in several states, and I desired to have a permanent location in the general area from which I could serve those who desired help. I travelled far, but the desire did not leave my mind. One evening, while in a hotel in Spokane, Washington, I relaxed completely on a couch, immobilized my attention, and in a quiet, passive manner imagined that I was talking to a large audience, saying in effect, "I am glad to be here; I have prayed for the ideal opportunity." I saw in my mind's eye the imaginary audience, and I felt the reality of it all. I played the role of the actor, dramatized this mental movie, and felt satisfied that this picture was being conveyed to my subconscious mind, which would bring it to pass in its own way. The next morning, on awakening, I felt a great sense of peace and satisfaction, and in a few days' time I received a telegram asking me to take over an organization in the Midwest, which I did, and I enjoyed it immensely for several years.

The method outlined here appeals to many who have de-scribed it as "the mental movie method." I have received numerous letters from people who listen to my radio talks and weekly public lectures, telling me of the wonderful results they get using this technique in the sale of their property. I suggest to those who have homes or property for sale that they satisfy themselves in their own mind that their price is right. Then, I claim that the Infinite Intelligence is attracting to them the buyer who really wants to have the property and who will love it and prosper in it. After having done this I suggest that they quiet their mind, relax, let go, and get into a drowsy, sleepy state, which reduces all mental effort to a minimum. Then, they are to picture the check in their hands, rejoice in the check, give thanks for the check, and go off to sleep feeling the naturalness of the whole mental movie created in their own mind. They must act as though it were an objective reality, and the subconscious mind will take it as an impression, and through the deeper currents of the mind the buyer and the seller are brought together. A mental picture held in the mind, backed by faith, will come to pass.

The Baudoin technique

Charles Baudoin was a professor at the Rousseau Institute in France. He was a brilliant psychotherapist and a research director of the New Nancy School of Healing, who in 1910 taught that the best way to impress the subconscious mind was to enter into a drowsy, sleepy state, or a state akin to sleep in which all effort was reduced to a minimum. Then in a quiet, passive, receptive way, by reflection, he would convey the idea to the subconscious.

The following is his formula: "A very simple way of securing this (impregnation of the subconscious mind) is to condense the idea which is to be the object of suggestion, to sum it up in a brief phrase which can be readily graven on the memory, and to repeat it over and over again as a lullaby."

Some years ago, a young lady in Los Angeles was engaged in a prolonged bitter family lawsuit over a will. Her husband had bequeathed his entire estate to her, and his sons and daughters by a previous marriage were bitterly fighting to break the will. The Baudoin technique was outlined to her, and this is what she did: She relaxed her body in an armchair, entered into the sleepy state and, as suggested, condensed the idea of her need into a phrase consisting of six words easily graven on the memory. "It is finished in Divine Order." The significance to her of these words meant that Infinite Intelligence operating through the laws of her subconscious mind would bring about a harmonious adjustment through the principle of harmony. She continued this procedure every night for about ten nights. After she got into a sleepy state, she would affirm slowly, quietly, and feelingly the statement: "It is finished in Divine Order," over and over again, feeling a sense of inner peace and an all-pervading tranquility; then she went off into her deep, normal sleep.

On the morning of the eleventh day, following the use of the above technique, she awakened with a sense of well-being, a conviction that *it was finished.* Her attorney called her the same day, saying that the opposing attorney and his clients were willing to settle. A harmonious agreement was reached, and litigation was discontinued.

The sleeping technique

By entering into a sleepy, drowsy state, effort is reduced to a minimum. The conscious mind is submerged to a great extent when in a sleepy state.

The reason for this is that the highest degree of outcropping of the subconscious occurs prior to sleep and just after we awaken. In this state the negative thoughts, which tend to neutralize your desire and so prevent acceptance by your subconscious mind, are no longer present.

Suppose you want to get rid of a destructive habit. Assume a comfortable posture, relax your body, and be still. Get into a sleepy state, and in that sleepy state, say quietly, over and over again as a lullaby, "I am completely free from this habit; harmony and peace of mind reign supreme." Repeat the above slowly, quietly, and lovingly for five or ten minutes, night and morning. Each time you repeat the words the emotional value becomes greater. When the urge comes to repeat the negative habit, repeat the above formula out loud by yourself. By this means you induce the subconscious to accept the idea, and a healing follows.

The thank-you technique

In the Bible, Paul recommends that we make known our requests with praise and thanksgiving. Some extraordinary results follow this simple method of prayer. The thankful heart is always close to the creative forces of the universe, causing countless blessings to flow toward it by the law of reciprocal relationship, based on a cosmic law of action and reaction.

For instance, a father promises his son a car for graduation; the boy has not yet received the car, but he is very thankful and happy, and is as joyous as though he has actually received the car. He knows his father will fulfil his promise, and he is full of gratitude and joy even though he has not yet received the car, objectively speaking. He has, however, received it with joy and thankfulness in his mind.

I shall illustrate how Mr. Broke applied this technique with excellent results. He said, "Bills are piling up, I am out of work, I have three children and no money. What shall I do?" Regularly every night and morning, for a period of about three weeks, he repeated the words, "Thank you, god, for my wealth," in a relaxed, peaceful manner until the feeling or mood of thankfulness dominated his mind. He imagined he was addressing the infinite power and intelligence within him knowing, of course, that he could not see the creative intelligence or infinite mind. He was seeing with the inner eye of spiritual perception, realizing that his thought-image of wealth was the *first cause*, relative to the money, position, and food he needed. His thought feeling was the substance of wealth, untrammelled by antecedent conditions of any kind. By repeating, "Thank you, god," over and over again, his mind and heart were lifted up to the point of acceptance, and when fear, thoughts of lack, poverty, and distress came into his mind, he would say, "Thank you, god," as often as necessary. He knew that as he kept up the thankful attitude, he would recondition his mind to the idea of wealth, which is what happened.

The sequel to his prayer is very interesting. After praying in the above-mentioned manner, he met a former employer of his on the street whom he had not seen for twenty years. The man offered him a very lucrative position and advanced him $500 on a temporary loan. Today, Mr. Broke is vice president of the company for which he works. His recent remark to me was, "I shall never forget the wonders of 'Thank you, god.' It has worked wonders for me."

The affirmative method

The effectiveness of an affirmation is determined largely by your understanding of the truth. Therefore, the power of your affirmation lies in the intelligent application of definite and specific positives. For example, a boy adds three and three and puts down seven on the blackboard. The teacher affirms with mathematical certainty that three and three are six; therefore, the boy changes his figures accordingly. The teacher's statement did not make three and three equal six because the latter was already a mathematical truth. The mathematical truth caused the boy to rearrange the figures on the blackboard. It is abnormal to be sick; it is normal to be healthy. Health is the truth of your being. When you affirm health, harmony, and peace for yourself or another, and when you realize these are universal principles of your own being, you will rearrange the negative patterns of your subconscious mind based on your faith and understanding of that which you affirm.

The result of the affirmative process of prayer depends on your conforming to the principles of life, regardless of appearances.

Consider for a moment that there is a principle of mathematics and none of error; there is a principle of truth but none of dishonesty.

There is a principle of intelligence but none of ignorance; there is a principle of harmony and none of discord. There is a principle of health but none of disease; and there is a principle of abundance but none of poverty.

The affirmative method was chosen by the author for use on his sister who was to be operated on for the removal of gall-stones in a hospital in England. The condition described was based on the diagnosis of hospital tests and the usual X-ray procedures. She asked me to pray for her. We were separated geographically about 6,500 miles, but there is no time or space in the mind principle. Infinite mind or intelligence is present in its entirety at every point simultaneously. I withdrew all thought from the contemplation of symptoms and from the corporeal personality altogether. I affirmed as follows: "This prayer is for my sister Catherine. She is relaxed and at peace, poised, balanced, serene, and calm. The healing intelligence of her subconscious mind, which created her body, is now transforming every cell, nerve, tissue, muscle, and bone of her being according to the perfect pattern of all organs lodged in her subconscious mind. Silently, quietly, all distorted thought patterns in her subconscious mind are removed and dissolved, and the vitality, wholeness, and beauty of the life principle are made manifest in every atom of her being. She is now open and receptive to the healing currents, which are flowing through her like a river, restoring her to perfect health, harmony, and peace. All distortions and ugly images are now washed away by the infinite ocean of love and peace flowing through her, and it is so."

I affirmed the above several times a day, and at the end of two weeks my sister had an examination, which showed a remarkable healing, and the X ray, proved negative.

To affirm is to state that it is so, and as you maintain this attitude of mind as true, regardless of all evidence to the contrary, you will receive an answer to your prayer. Your thought can only affirm, for even if you deny something, you are actually affirming the presence of what you deny.

Repeating an affirmation, knowing what you are saying and why you are saying it, leads the mind to that state of consciousness where it accepts that which you state as true. Keep on affirming the truths of life until you get the subconscious reaction, which satisfies.

The argumentative method

This method is just what the word implies. It stems from the procedure of Dr. Phineas Parkhurst Quimby of Maine. Dr. Quimby, a pioneer in mental and spiritual healing, lived and practiced in Belfast, Maine, about one hundred years ago. A book called *The Quimby Manuscripts,* published in 1921 gives newspaper accounts of this man's remarkable results in prayer treatment of the sick.

Quimby duplicated many of the healing miracles. In brief, the argumentative method employed according to Quimby consists of spiritual reasoning where you convince the patient and yourself that his sickness is due to his false belief, groundless fears, and negative patterns lodged in his subconscious mind. You reason it out clearly in your mind and convince your patient that the disease or ailment is due only to a distorted, twisted pattern of thought, which has taken form in his body. This wrong belief in some external power and external causes has now externalized itself as sickness, and can be changed by changing the thought patterns.

You explain to the sick person that the basis of all healing is a change of belief. You also point out that the subconscious mind created the body and all its organs; therefore, it knows how to heal it, can heal it, and is doing so now as you speak. You argue in the courtroom of your mind that the disease is a shadow of the mind based on disease-soaked, morbid thought-imagery.

You continue to build up all the evidence you can muster on behalf of the healing power within, which created all the organs in the first place, and which has a perfect pattern of every cell, nerve, and tissue within it. Then, you render a verdict in the courthouse of your mind in favor of yourself or your patient. You liberate the sick one by faith and spiritual understanding. Your mental and spiritual evidence is overwhelming; they're being but one mind, what you feel as true will be resurrected in the experience of the patient. This procedure is essentially the argumentative method used by Dr. Quimby of Maine from 1849 to 1869.

The absolute method is like modern sound wave therapy

Many people throughout the world practice this form of prayer treatment with wonderful results. The person using the absolute method mentions the name of the patient, such as John Jones, then quietly and silently thinks of God and His qualities and attributes, such as, God is all bliss, boundless love, infinite intelligence, all-powerful, boundless wisdom, absolute harmony, indescribable beauty, and perfection. As he quietly thinks along these lines, he is lifted up in consciousness into a new spiritual wave length, at which times he feels the infinite ocean of god's love is now dissolving everything unlike itself in the mind and body of John Jones for whom he is praying. He feels all the power and love of god are now focused on John Jones, and whatever is bothering or vexing him is now completely neutralized in the presence of the infinite ocean of life and love.

The absolute method of prayer might be likened to the sound wave or sonic therapy recently shown me by a distinguished physician in Los Angeles. He has an ultra sound wave machine, which oscillates at a tremendous speed and sends sound waves to any area of the body to which it is directed. These sound waves can be controlled, and he told me of achieving remarkable results in dissolving arthritic calcareous deposits, as well as the healing and removal of other disturbing conditions.

To the degree that we rise in consciousness by contemplating qualities and attributes of God, do we generate spiritual electronic waves of harmony, health, and peace. Many remarkable healings follow this technique of prayer.

The decree method

Power goes into our word according to the feeling and faith behind it. When we realize the power that moves the world is moving on our behalf and is backing up our word, our confidence and assurance grow. You do not try and add power to power; therefore, there must be no mental striving, coercion, force, or mental wrestling.

A young girl used the decree method on a young man who was constantly phoning her, pressing her for dates, and meeting her at her place of business; she found it very difficult to get rid of him. She decreed as follows: "I release... unto God. He is in his true place at all times. I am free, and he is free. I now decree that my words go forth into infinite mind and it brings it to pass. It is so." She said he vanished and she has never seen him since, adding, "It was as though the ground swallowed him up."

Serve yourself with scientific truth

Be a mental engineer and use tried and proven techniques in building a grander and greater life.

Your desire is your prayer. Picture the fulfillment of your desire now and feel its reality, and you will experience the joy of the answered prayer.

Desire to accomplish things the easy way – with the sure aid of mental science.

You can build radiant health, success, and happiness by the thoughts you think in the hidden studio of your mind.

Experiment scientifically until you personally prove that there is always a direct response from the infinite intelligence of your subconscious mind to your conscious thinking.

Feel the joy and restfulness in foreseeing the certain accomplishment of your desire. Any mental picture, which you have in your mind, is the substance of things hoped for and the evidence of things not seen.

A mental picture is worth a thousand words. Your subconscious will bring to pass any picture held in the mind backed by faith.

Avoid all effort or mental coercion in prayer. Get into a sleepy, drowsy state and lull yourself to sleep feeling and knowing that your prayer is answered.

Remember that the thankful heart is always close to the riches of the universe.

To affirm is to state that it is so, and as you maintain this attitude of mind as true, regardless of all evidence to the contrary, you will receive an answer to your prayer.

Generate electronic waves of harmony, health, and peace by thinking of the love and the glory of god.

What you decree and feel as true will come to pass. Decree harmony, health, peace, and abundance.

4

HOW YOUR SUBCONSCIOUS
REMOVES MENTAL BLOCKS

The solution lies within the problem. The answer is in every question. If you are presented with a difficult situation and you cannot see your way clear, the best procedure is to assume that infinite intelligence within your subconscious mind knows all and sees all, has the answer, and is revealing it to you now. Your new mental attitude that the creative intelligence is bringing about a happy solution will enable you to find the answer. Rest assured that such an attitude of mind would bring order, peace, and meaning to all your undertakings.

How to break or build a habit

You are a creature of habit. Habit is the function of your subconscious mind. You learned to swim, ride a bicycle, dance, and drive a car by consciously doing these things over and over again until they established tracks in your subconscious mind. Then, the automatic habit action of your subconscious mind took over. This is sometimes called second nature, which is a reaction of your subconscious mind to your thinking and acting.

You are free to choose a good habit or a bad habit. If you repeat a negative thought or act over a period of time, you will be under the compulsion of a habit. The law of your subconscious is compulsion.

How he broke a bad habit

Mr. Jones said to me, "An uncontrollable urge to drink seizes me, and I remain drunk for two weeks at a time. I can't give up this terrible habit."

Time and time again these experiences had occurred to this unfortunate man. He had grown into the habit of drinking to excess. Although he had started drinking of his own initiative, he also began to realize that he could change the habit and establish a new one. He said that while through his will power he was able to suppress his desires temporarily, his continued efforts to suppress the many urges only made matters worse. His repeated failures convinced him that he was hopeless and powerless to control his urge or obsession. This idea of being powerless operated as a powerful suggestion to his subconscious mind and aggravated his weakness, making his life a succession of failures.

I taught him to harmonize the functions of the conscious and subconscious mind. When these two cooperate, the idea or desire implanted in the subconscious mind is realized. His reasoning mind agreed that if the old habit path or track had carried him into trouble, he could consciously form a new path to freedom, sobriety, and peace of mind. He knew that his destructive habit was automatic, but since it was acquired through his conscious choice, he realized that if he had been conditioned negatively, he also could be conditioned positively. As a result, he ceased thinking of the fact that he was powerless to overcome the habit. Moreover, he understood clearly that there was no obstacle to his healing other than his own thought.

Therefore, there was no occasion for great mental effort or mental coercion.

The power of his mental picture

This man acquired a practice of relaxing his body and getting into a relaxed, drowsy, meditative state. Then he filled his mind with the picture of the desired end, knowing his subconscious mind could bring it about the easiest way. He imagined his daughter congratulating him on his freedom, and saying to him, "Daddy, it's wonderful to have you home!" He had lost his family through drink. He was not allowed to visit them, and his wife would not speak to him.

Regularly, systematically, he used to sit down and meditate in the way outlined. When his attention wandered, he made it a habit to immediately recall the mental picture of his daughter with her smile and the scene of his home enlivened by her cheerful voice. All this brought about a reconditioning of his mind. It was a gradual process. He kept it up. He persevered knowing that sooner or later, he would establish a new habit pattern in his subconscious mind.

I told him that he could liken his conscious mind to a camera, that his subconscious mind was the sensitive plate on which he registered and impressed the picture. This made a profound impression on him, and his whole aim was to firmly impress the picture on his mind and develop it there. Films are developed in the dark; likewise, mental pictures are developed in the darkroom of the subconscious mind.

Focused attention

Realizing that his conscious mind was simply a camera, he used no effort. There was no mental struggle. He quietly adjusted his thoughts and focused his attention on the scene before him until he gradually became identified with the picture. He became absorbed in the mental atmosphere, repeating the mental movie frequently. There was no room for doubt that a healing would follow. When there was any temptation to drink, he would switch his imagination from any reveries of drinking bouts to the feeling of being at home with his family. He was successful because he confidently expected to experience the picture he was developing in his mind. Today he is the president of a multimillion-dollar concern and is radiantly happy.

He said a jinx was following him

Mr. Block said that he had been making an annual income of $20,000, but for the past three months all doors seemed to jam tightly. He brought clients up to the point where they were about to sign on the dotted line, and then at the eleventh hour the door closed. He added that perhaps a jinx was following him.

In discussing the matter with Mr. Block, I discovered that three months previously, he had become very irritated, annoyed, and resentful toward a dentist who, after he had promised to sign a contract, had withdrawn at the last moment. He began to live in the unconscious fear that other clients would do the same, thereby setting up a history of frustration, hostility, and obstacles. He gradually built up in his mind a belief in obstruction and last minute cancellations until a vicious circle had been established. *What I fear most has come upon me.* Mr. Block realized that the trouble was in his mind, and that it was essential to change his mental attitude.

His run of so-called misfortune was broken in the following way: "I realize I am one with the infinite intelligence of my subconscious mind which knows no obstacle, difficulty, or delay. I live in the joyous expectancy of the best. My deeper mind responds to my thoughts. I know that the work of the infinite power of my subconscious cannot be hindered. Infinite intelligence always finishes successfully whatever it begins. Creative wisdom works through me, bringing all my plans and purposes to completion. Whatever I start, I bring to a successful conclusion. My aim in life is to give wonderful service, and all those whom I contact are blessed by what I have to offer. All my work comes to full fruition in divine order."

He repeated this prayer every morning before going to call on his customers, and he also prayed each night prior to sleep. In a short time he had established a new habit pattern in his subconscious mind, and he was back in his old accustomed stride as a successful salesman.

How much do you want what you want?

A young man asked Socrates how he could get wisdom. Socrates replied, "Come with me." He took the lad to a river, pushed the boy's head under the water, held it there until the boy was gasping for air, then relaxed and released his head. When the boy regained his composure, he asked him, "What did you desire most when you were under water?"

"I wanted air," said the boy.

Socrates said to him, "When you want wisdom as much as you wanted air when you were immersed in the water, you will receive it."

Likewise, when you really have an intense desire to overcome any block in your life, and you come to a clear-cut decision that there is a way out, and that is the course you wish to follow, then victory and triumph are assured.

If you really want peace of mind and inner calm, you will get it. Regardless of how unjustly you have been treated, or how unfair the boss has been, or what a mean scoundrel someone has proved to be, all this makes no difference to you when you awaken to your mental and spiritual powers. You know what you want, and you will definitely refuse to let the thieves (thoughts) of hatred, anger, hostility, and ill will rob you of peace, harmony, health, and happiness. You cease to become upset by people, conditions, news, and events by identifying your thoughts immediately with your aim in life. Your aim is peace, health, inspiration, harmony, and abundance. Feel a river of peace flowing through you now. Your thought is the immaterial and invisible power, and you choose to let it bless, inspire, and give you peace.

Why he could not be healed

This is a case history of a married man with four children who was supporting and secretly living with another woman during his business trips.

He was ill, nervous, irritable, and cantankerous, and he could not sleep without drugs. The doctor's medicine failed to bring down his high blood pressure of over two hundred. He had pains in numerous organs of his body, which doctors could not diagnose or relieve. To make matters worse, he was drinking heavily.

The cause of all this was a deep unconscious sense of guilt. He had violated the marriage vows, and this troubled him. The religious creed he was brought up on was deeply lodged in his subconscious mind, and he drank excessively to heal the wound of guilt. Some invalids take morphine and codeine for severe pains;

he was taking alcohol for the pain or wound in his mind. It was the old story of adding fuel to the fire.

The explanation and the cure

He listened to the explanation of how his mind worked. He faced his problem, looked at it, and gave up his dual role. He knew that his drinking was an unconscious attempt to escape. The hidden cause lodged in his subconscious mind had to be eradicated; then the healing would follow.

He began to impress his subconscious mind three or four times a day by using the following prayer: "My mind is full of peace, poise, balance, and equilibrium. The infinite lies stretched in smiling repose within me. I am not afraid of anything in the past, the present, or the future. The infinite intelligence of my subconscious mind leads, guides, and directs me in all ways. I now meet every situation with faith, poise, calmness, and confidence.

"I am now completely free from the habit. My mind is full of inner peace, freedom, and joy. I forgive myself; then I am forgiven. Peace, sobriety, and confidence reign supreme in my mind."

He repeated this prayer frequently as outlined; being fully aware of what he was doing and why he was doing it. Knowing what he was doing gave him the necessary faith and confidence. I explained to him that as he spoke these statements out loud, slowly, lovingly, and meaningfully, they would gradually sink down into his subconscious mind. Like seeds, they would grow after their kind. These truths, on which he concentrated, went in through his eyes, his ears heard the sound, and the healing vibrations of these words reached his subconscious mind and obliterated all the negative mental patterns which caused all the trouble. Light dispels darkness. The constructive thought destroys the negative thought. He became a transformed man within a month.

Refusing to admit it

If you are an alcoholic or drug addict, admit it. Do not dodge the issue. Many people remain alcoholics because they refuse to admit it.

Your disease is instability, an inner fear. You are refusing to face life, and so you try to escape your responsibilities through the bottle. As an alcoholic you have no free will, although you think you have, and you may even boast about your will power. If you are a habitual drunkard and say bravely, "I will not touch it anymore," you have no power to make this assertion come true, because you do not know where to locate the power.

You are living in a psychological prison of your own making, and you are bound by your beliefs, opinions, training, and environmental influences.

Like most people, you are a creature of habit. You are conditioned to react the way you do.

Building in the idea of freedom

You can build the idea of freedom and peace of mind into your mentality so that it reaches your subconscious depths. The latter, being all powerful, will free you from all desire for alcohol. Then, you will have the new understanding of how your mind works, and you can truly back up your statement and prove the truth to yourself.

Fifty-one percent healed

If you have a keen desire to free yourself from any destructive habit, you are fifty-one percent healed already. When you have a greater desire to give up the bad habit than to continue it, you will not experience too much difficulty in gaining complete freedom.

Whatever thought you anchor the mind upon, the latter magnifies. If you engage the mind on the concept of freedom (freedom from the habit) and peace of mind, and if you keep it focused on this new direction of attention, you generate feelings and emotions, which gradually emotionalize the concept of freedom and peace. Whatever idea you emotionalize is accepted by your subconscious and brought to pass.

The law of substitution

Realize that something good can come out of your suffering. You have not suffered in vain. However, it is foolish to continue to suffer.

If you continue as an alcoholic, it will bring about mental and physical deterioration and decay. Realize that the power in your subconscious is backing you up. Even though you may be seized with melancholia, you should begin to imagine the joy of freedom that is in store for you. This is the law of substitution. Your imagination took you to the bottle; let it take you now to freedom and peace of mind. You will suffer a little bit, but it is for a constructive purpose. You will bear it like a mother in the pangs of childbirth, and you will, likewise, bring forth a child of the mind. Your subconscious will give birth to sobriety.

Cause of alcoholism

The real cause of alcoholism is negative and destructive thinking; for as a man thinketh, so is he. The alcoholic has a deep sense of inferiority, inadequacy, defeat, and frustration, usually accompanied by a deep inner hostility. He has countless alibis as to his reason for drinking, but the sole reason is in his *thought life.*

Three magic steps

The first step: Get still; quiet the wheels of the mind. Enter into a sleepy, drowsy state. In this relaxed, peaceful, receptive state, you are preparing for the second step.

The second step: Take a brief phrase, which can readily be graven on the memory, and repeat it over and over as a lullaby. Use the phrase, "Sobriety and peace of mind are mine now, and I give thanks." To prevent the mind from wandering, repeat it aloud or sketch its pronunciation with the lips and tongue as you say it mentally. This helps its entry into the subconscious mind. Do this for five minutes or more. You will find a deep emotional response.

The third step: Just before going to sleep, practice what Johann von Goethe, German author, used to do. Imagine a friend, a loved one in front of you. Your eyes are closed, you are relaxed and at peace. The loved one or friend is subjectively present, and is saying to you, "Congratulations!" You see the smile; you hear the voice. You mentally touch the hand; it is all real and vivid. The word *congratulations* imply complete freedom. Hear it over and over again until you get the sub-conscious reaction, which satisfies.

Keep on keeping on

When fear knocks at the door of your mind, or when worry, anxiety, and doubt cross your mind, behold your vision, your goal. Think of the infinite power within your subconscious mind, which you can generate by your thinking and imagining, and this will give you confidence, power, and courage. Keep on, persevere, *until the day breaks, and the shadows fly away.*

Review your thought power

The solution lies within the problem. The answer is in every question. Infinite intelligence responds to you as you call upon it with faith and confidence.

Habit is the function of your subconscious mind. There is no greater evidence of the marvellous power of your subconscious than the force and sway habit holds in your life. You are a creature of habit.

You form habit patterns in your subconscious mind by repeating a thought and act over and over again until it establishes tracks in the subconscious mind and becomes automatic, such as swimming, dancing, typing, walking, driving your car, etc.

You have freedom to choose. You can choose a good habit or a bad habit. Prayer is a good habit.

Whatever mental picture, backed by faith, you behold in your conscious mind, your subconscious mind will bring to pass.

The only obstacle to your success and achievement is your own thought or mental image.

When your attention wanders, bring it back to the contemplation of your good or goal. Make a habit of this. This is called disciplining the mind.

Your conscious mind is the camera, and your subconscious mind is the sensitive plate on which you register or impress the picture.

The only jinx that follows anyone is a fear thought repeated over and over in the mind. Break the jinx by knowing that whatever you start, you will bring to a conclusion in divine order. Picture the happy ending and sustain it with confidence.

To form a new habit, you must be convinced that it is desirable. When your desire to give up the bad habit is greater than your desire to continue, you are fifty-one percent healed already.

The statements of others cannot hurt you, except through your own thoughts and mental participation. Identify yourself with your aim, which is peace, harmony and joy. You are the only thinker in your universe.

Excessive drinking is an unconscious desire to escape. The cause of alcoholism is negative and destructive thinking. The cure is to think of freedom, sobriety, and perfection, and to feel the thrill of accomplishment.

Many people remain alcoholics because they refuse to admit it.

The law of your subconscious mind, which held you in bondage and inhibited your freedom of action, will give you freedom and happiness. It depends on how you use it.

Your imagination took you to the vice; let it take you to freedom by imagining you are free.

When fear knocks at the door of your mind, let faith in god and all things good open the door.

5

HOW TO STAY YOUNG
IN SPIRIT FOREVER

Your subconscious mind never grows old. It is timeless, ageless, and endless. It is a part of the universal mind of god, which was never born, and it will never die.

Fatigue or old age cannot be predicated on any spiritual quality or power. Patience, kindness, veracity, humility, good will, peace, harmony, and brotherly love are attributes and qualities, which never grow old. If you continue to generate these qualities here on this plane of life, you will always remain young in spirit.

I remember reading an article in one of our magazines some years ago, which stated that a group of eminent medical men at the clinic in reported that years alone are not responsible for bringing about degenerative disorders. These same physicians stated that it is the fear of time, not time itself, that has a harmful aging effect on our minds and bodies, and that the neurotic fear of the effects of time may well be the cause of premature aging.

During the many years of my public life, I have had occasion to study the biographies of the famous men and women who have continued their productive activities into the years well beyond the normal span of life.

Some of them achieve their greatness in old age. At the same time, it has been my privilege to meet and to know countless individuals of no prominence who, in their lesser sphere, belonged to those hardy mortals who have proved that old age does not destroy the creative powers of the mind and body.

He had grown old in his thought life

A few years ago I called on an old friend in London. He was over 80 years of age, very ill, and obviously was yielding to his advancing years. Our conversation revealed his physical weakness, his sense of frustration, and a general deterioration almost approaching lifelessness. His cry was that he was useless and that no one wanted him. With an expression of hopelessness he betrayed his false philosophy, "We are born, grow up, become old, good for nothing, and that's the end."

This mental attitude of futility and worthlessness was the chief reason for his sickness. He was looking forward only to senescence, and after that – nothing. Indeed, he had grown old in his thought life, and his subconscious mind brought about all the evidence of his habitual thinking.

Age is the dawn of wisdom

Unfortunately, many people have the same attitude as this unhappy man. They are afraid of what they term "old age," the end, and extinction, which really means that they are afraid of life. Yet, life is endless. Age is not the flight of years, but the dawn of wisdom.

Wisdom is an awareness of the tremendous spiritual powers in your subconscious mind and the knowledge of how to apply these powers to lead a full and happy life. Get it out of your head once and for all that 65, 75, or 85 years of age is synonymous with the end for you or anybody else. It can be the beginning of a glorious, fruitful, active, and most productive life pattern, better than you have ever experienced. Believe this, expect it, and your subconscious will bring it to pass.

Welcome the change

Old age is not a tragic occurrence. What we call the aging process is really change. It is to be welcomed joyfully and gladly as each phase of human life is a step forward on the path, which has no end. Man has powers, which transcend his bodily powers. He has senses, which transcend his five physical senses.

Scientists today are finding positive indisputable evidence that something conscious in man can leave his present body and travel thousands of miles to see, hear, touch, and speak to people even though his physical body never leaves the couch on which it reclines.

Man's life is spiritual and eternal. He need never grow old for life, or god, cannot grow old. Life is self-renewing, eternal, indestructible, and is the reality of all men.

Evidence for survival

The evidence gathered by the psychical research societies, both in Great Britain and America is overwhelming. You may go into any large metropolitan library and get volumes on *The Proceedings of the Psychical Research Society* based on findings of distinguished scientists on survival following so-called death. You will find a startling report on scientific experiments establishing the reality of life after death in *The Case for Psychic Survival* by Hereward Carrington, Director of the American Psychical Institute.

Life is

A woman asked Thomas Edison, the electrical wizard, "Mr. Edison, what is electricity?"

He replied, "Madame, electricity is. Use it."

Electricity is a name we give an invisible power which we do not fully comprehend, but we learn all we can about the principle of electricity and its uses. We use it in countless ways.

The scientist cannot see an electron with his eyes, yet he accepts it as a scientific fact, because it is the only valid conclusion, which coincides with his other experimental evidence. We cannot see life. However, we know we are alive. Life is, and we are here to express it in all its beauty and glory.

Mind and spirit do not grow old

The man who thinks or believes that the earthly cycle of birth, adolescence, youth, maturity, and old age is all there is to life, is indeed to be pitied. Such a man has no anchor, no hope, no vision, and to him life has no meaning.

This type of belief brings frustration, stagnation, cynicism, and a sense of hopelessness resulting in neurosis and mental aberrations of all kinds. If you cannot play a fast game of tennis, or swim as fast as your son, or if your body has slowed down, or you walk with a slow step, remember life is always clothing itself anew. What men call death is but a journey to a new city in another dimension of life.

I say to men and women in my lectures that they should accept what we call old age gracefully. Age has its own glory, beauty, and wisdom, which belong to it. Peace, love, joy, beauty, happiness, wisdom, good will, and understanding are qualities, which never grow old or die.

Ralph Waldo Emerson, poet and philosopher, said, "We do not count a man's years until he has nothing else to count."

Your character, the quality of your mind, your faith, and your convictions are not subject to decay.

You are as young as you think you are

I give public lectures in Caxton Hall, London, England, every few years, and following one of these lectures, a surgeon said to me, "I am 84 years of age. I operate every morning, visit patients in the afternoons, and I write for medical and other scientific journals in the evening."

His attitude was that he was as useful as he believed himself to be, and that he was as young as his thoughts. He said to me, "It's true what you said, 'Man is as strong as he thinks he is, and as valuable as he thinks he is.'"

This surgeon has not surrendered to advancing years. He knows that he is immortal. His final comment to me was, "If I should pass on tomorrow, I would be operating on people in the next dimension, not with a surgeon's scalpel, but with mental and spiritual surgery."

Your gray hairs are an asset

Don't ever quit a job and say, "I am retired; I am old; I am finished." That would be stagnation, death, and you would be finished. Some men are old at 30, while others are young at 80. The mind is the master weaver, the architect, the designer, and the sculptor. George Bernard Shaw was active at 90, and the artistic quality of his mind had not relaxed from active duty.

I meet men and women who tell me that some employers almost slam the door in their faces when they say they are over 40. This attitude on the part of the employers is to be considered cold, callous, evil, and completely void of compassion and understanding. The total emphasis seems to be on youth, i.e. you must be under 35 years of age to receive consideration. The reasoning behind this is certainly very shallow. If the employer would stop and think, he would realize that the man or woman was not selling his age or gray hair, rather, he was willing to give of his talents, his experience, and his wisdom gathered through years of experience in the market place of life.

Age is an asset
Your age should be a distinct asset to any organization, because of your practice and application through the years of the principles of the Golden Rule and the law of love and good will. Your gray hair, if you have any, should stand for greater wisdom, skill, and understanding. Your emotional and spiritual maturity should be a tremendous blessing to any organization.

A man should not be asked to resign when he is 65 years of age. That is the time of life when he could be most useful in handling personnel problems, making plans for the future, making decisions, and guiding others in the realm of creative ideas based on his experience and insight into the nature of the business.

Be your age
A motion-picture writer in Hollywood told me that he had to write scripts, which would cater to the twelve-year-old mind.

This is a tragic state of affairs if the great masses of people are expected to become emotionally and spiritually mature. It means that the emphasis is placed on youth in spite of the fact that youth stands for inexperience, lack of discernment, and hasty judgment.

I can keep up with the best of them

I am now thinking of a man 65 years of age who is trying frantically to keep young. He swims with young men every Sunday, goes on long hikes, plays tennis, and boasts of his prowess and physical powers, saying, "Look, I can keep up with the best of them!"

He should remember the great truth: *As a man thinketh in his heart, so is he.*

Diets, exercises, and games of all kinds will not keep this man young. It is necessary for him to observe that he grows old or remains young in accordance with his processes of thinking. Your subconscious mind is conditioned by your thoughts. If your thoughts are constantly on the beautiful, the noble, and the good, you will remain young regardless of the chronological years.

Fear of old age

Job said, *The thing which I greatly feared is come upon me.* There are many people who fear old age and are uncertain about the future, because they anticipate mental and physical deterioration as the years advance. What they think and feel comes to pass.

You grow old when you lose interest in life, when you cease to dream, to hunger after new truths, and to search for new worlds to conquer. When your mind is open to new ideas, new interests, and when you raise the curtain and let in the sunshine and inspiration of new truths of life and the universe, you will be young and vital.

You have much to give

If you are 65 or 95 years of age, realize you have much to give. You can help stabilize, advise, and direct the younger generation. You can give the benefit of your knowledge, your experience, and your wisdom. You can always look ahead for at all times you are gazing into infinite life. You will find that you can never cease to unveil the glories and wonders of life. Try to learn something new every moment of the day, and you will find your mind will always be young.

One hundred and ten years old

Some years ago while lecturing in Bombay, India, I was introduced to a man who said he was 110 years old. He had the most beautiful face I have ever seen. He seemed transfigured by the radiance of an inner light. There was a rare beauty in his eyes indicating he had grown old in years with gladness and with no indication that his mind had dimmed its lights.

Retirement is a new venture

Be sure that your mind never retires. It must be like a parachute, which is no good unless it opens up. Be open and receptive to new ideas. I have seen men of 65 and 70 retire. They seemed to rot away, and in a few months passed on. They obviously felt that life was at an end.

Retirement can be a new venture, a new challenge, a new path, the beginning of the fulfillment of a long dream. It is inexpressibly depressing to hear a man say, "What shall I do now that I am retired?" He is saying in effect, "I am mentally and physically dead. My mind is bankrupt of ideas."

All this is a false picture. The real truth is that you can accomplish more at 90 than you did at 60, because each day you are growing in wisdom and understanding of life and the

Secret of youth

To recapture the days of your youth, feel the miraculous, healing, self renewing power of your subconscious mind moving through your whole being. Know and feel that you are inspired, lifted up, rejuvenated, revitalized, and recharged spiritually. You can bubble over with enthusiasm and joy, as in the days of your youth, for the simple reason that you can always mentally and emotionally recapture the joyous state.

The candle, which shines upon your head, is divine intelligence, and reveals to you everything you need to know; it enables you to affirm the presence of your good, regardless of appearances. You walk by the guidance of your subconscious mind, because you know that the dawn appears and the shadows flee away.

Get a vision

Instead of saying, "I am old," say, "I am wise in the way of the Divine Life." Don't let the corporation, newspapers, or statistics hold a picture before you of old age, declining years, decrepitude, senility, and uselessness. Reject it, for it is a lie. Refuse to be hypnotized by such propaganda. Affirm life – not death. Get a vision of yourself as happy, radiant, successful, serene, and powerful.

Your mind does not grow old

Former President Herbert Hoover was very active in performing monumental work even in his late eighties. I interviewed him a few years ago in New York City. I found him healthy, happy, vigorous, and full of life and enthusiasm. He was keeping several secretaries busy handling his correspondence and was himself writing books of a political and historical nature. Like all great men, I found him affable, genial, amiable, loving, and most understanding.

His mental acumen and sagacity gave me the thrill of a lifetime. He is a deeply religious man, and is full of faith in God and in the triumph of the eternal truth of life. He was subjected to a barrage of criticism and condemnation in the years of the great depression, but he weathered the storm and did not grow old in hatred, resentment, ill will, and bitterness. On the contrary, he went into the silence of his soul, and communing with the Divine Presence within him, he found the peace, which is the power at the heart of god.

His mind active at ninety-nine

My father learned the French language at 65 years of age, and became an authority on it at 70. He made a study of Gaelic when he was over 60, and became an acknowledged and famous teacher of the subject. He assisted my sister in a school of higher learning and continued to do so until he passed away at 99. His mind was as clear at 99 as it was when he was 20. Moreover, his handwriting and his reasoning powers had improved with age. Truly, you are as old as you think and feel.

We need our senior citizens

Marcus Porcius Cato, the Roman patriot, learned Greek at 80. Madame Ernestine Schumann-Heink, the great German-American contralto, reached the pinnacle of her musical success after she became a grandmother. It is wonderful to behold the accomplishments of the oldsters. General Douglas Mac-Arthur, Harry S. Truman, General Dwight David Eisenhower, and American financier Bernard Baruch are interesting, active, and contributing their talents and wisdom to the world.

The Greek philosopher Socrates, learned to play musical instruments when he was 80 years old. Michelangelo was painting his greatest canvases at 80. At 80, Cios Simonides won the prize for poetry, Johann von Goethe finished *Faust,* and Leopold von Ranke commenced his *History of the World,* which he finished at 92.

Alfred Tennyson wrote a magnificent poem, "Crossing the Bar," at 83.

Isaac Newton was hard at work close to 85. At 88 John Wesley was directing, preaching, and guiding Methodism. We have several men of 95 years who come to my lectures, and they tell me they are in better health now than they were at 20.

Let us place our senior citizens in high places and give them every opportunity to bring forth the flowers of Paradise.

If you are retired, get interested in the laws of life and the wonders of your subconscious mind. Do something you have always wanted to do. Study new subjects, and investigate new ideas.

Profitable pointers

1. Patience, kindness, love, good will, joy, happiness, wisdom, and understanding are qualities, which never grow old. Cultivate them and express them, and remain young in mind and body.

2. Some research physicians say that the neurotic fear of the effects of time may well be the cause of premature aging.

3. Age is not the flight of years; it is the dawn of wisdom in the mind of man.

4. The most productive years of your life can be from 65 to 95.

5. Welcome the advancing years. It means you are moving higher on the path of life, which has no end.

6. Life is self-renewing, eternal, and indestructible, and is the reality of all men. You live forever, because your life is god's life.

7. Evidence of survival after death is overwhelming. Study *Proceedings of Psychical Research Society of Great Britain and America* in your library. Outstanding scientists base the work on the scientific research for over 75 years.

8. You cannot see your mind, but you know you have a mind. You cannot see spirit, but you know that the spirit of the game, the spirit of the artist, the spirit of the musician, and the spirit of

the speaker is real. Likewise, the spirit of goodness, truth, and beauty moving in your mind and heart are real. You cannot see life, but you know you are alive.

9. Old age may be called the contemplation of the truths of god from the highest standpoint. The joys of old age are greater than those of youth. Your mind is engaged in spiritual and mental athletics. Nature slows down your body so that you may have the opportunity to meditate on things divine.

10. We do not count a man's years until he has nothing else to count. Your faith and convictions are not subject to decay.

11. You are as young as you think you are. You are as strong as you think you are. You are as useful as you think you are. You are as young as your thoughts.

12. Your gray hair is an asset. You are not selling your gray hairs. You are selling your talent, abilities, and wisdom, which you have garnered through the years.

13. Diets and exercises won't keep you young. *As a man thinketh, so is he.*

14. Fear of old age can bring about physical and mental deterioration. *The thing I greatly feared has come upon me.*

15. You grow old when you cease to dream, and when you lose interest in life. You grow old if you are irritable, crotchety, petulant, and cantankerous. Fill your mind with the truths of god and radiate the sunshine of his love – this is youth.

16. Look ahead, for at all times you are gazing into infinite life.

17. Your retirement is a new venture. Take up new studies and new

interests. You can now do the things you always wanted to do when you were so busy making a living. Give your attention to living life.

18. Become a producer and not a prisoner of society. Don't hide your light.

19. The secret of youth is love, joy, inner peace, and laughter. *In Him there is fullness of joy. In Him there is no darkness at all.*

20. You are needed. Some of the great philosophers, artists, scientists, writers, and others accomplished their greatest work after they were 80 years old.

21. The fruits of old age are love, joy, peace, patience, gentleness, goodness, faith, meekness, and temperance.

22. You are a son of Infinite Life, which knows no end. You are a child of eternity. You are wonderful!

HOW TO STOP WORRYING
AND START LIVING

Dale Carnegie

1

A MAGIC FORMULA FOR SOLVING
WORRY SITUATIONS

Would you like a quick, sure-fire recipe for handling worry situations, a technique you can start using right away, before you go any further in reading this book? Then let me tell you about the method worked out by Willis H. Carrier, the brilliant engineer who launched the air-conditioning industry, head of the world-famous Carrier Corporation in New York. It is one of the best techniques I ever heard of for solving worry problems.

Mr. Carrier said,

> When I was a young man, I worked for the Buffalo Forge Company in New York. I was handed the assignment of installing a gas-cleaning device in a plant of the Pittsburgh

Plate Glass Company at Crystal City, Missouri – plant costing millions of dollars. The purpose of this installation was to remove the impurities from the gas so it could be burned without injuring the engines. This method of cleaning gas was new. It had been tried only once before and under different conditions. In my work at Crystal City, Missouri, unforeseen difficulties arose. It worked after a fashion – but not well enough to meet the guarantee we had made.

I was stunned by my failure. It was almost as if someone had struck me a blow on the head. My stomach and my insides began to twist and turn. For a while I was so worried I couldn't sleep.

Finally, common sense reminded me that worry wasn't getting me anywhere; so I figured out a way to handle my problem without worrying. It worked perfectly. I have been using this same anti-worry technique for more than thirty years.

It is simple. Anyone can use it. It consists of three steps:

Step I: I analyzed the situation fearlessly and honestly and figure out what was the worst that could possibly happen as a result of this failure. No one was going to jail me or shoot me. That was certain. True, there was a chance that I would lose my position; and there was also a chance that my employers would have to remove the machinery and lose the twenty thousand dollars we had invested.

Step II: After figuring out what was the worst that could possibly happen, I reconciled myself to accepting it if necessary. I said to myself: This failure will be a blow to my record, and it might possibly mean the loss of my job; however, if it does, I can always get another position. Conditions could be much worse; and as far as my employers are concerned, well, they that we are experimenting with a new method of cleaning gas, and if this experience costs them twenty thousand dollars, they can stand it. They can charge it up to research, for it is an experiment.

After discovering the worst that could possibly happen and reconciling myself to accepting it, if necessary, an extremely important thing happened: I immediately relaxed and felt a sense of peace that I hadn't experienced in days.

Step III: From that time on, I calmly devoted my time and energy to try and improve upon the worst which I had already accepted mentally.

I now tried to figure out ways and means by which I might reduce the loss of twenty thousand dollars that we faced. I made several tests and finally figured out that if we spent another five thousand for additional equipment, our problem would be solved. We did it, and instead of the firm losing twenty thousand, we made fifteen thousand."

I probably would never have been able to do this if I had kept on worrying, because one of the worst features about worrying is that it destroys our ability to concentrate. When we worry, our minds jump here and there and everywhere, and we lose all power of decision. However, when we force ourselves to face the worst and accept it mentally, we then eliminate all those vague imaginations and put ourselves in a position, where we are able to concentrate on our problem,

This incident that I have related occurred many years ago. It worked so superbly that I have been using it ever since; and, as a result, my life has been almost free from worry.

Now, why is Willis H. Carrier's magic formula so valuable and so practical, psychologically speaking? Because it yanks us down out of the great grey clouds in which we fumble around when we are blinded by worry. It plants our feet good and solid on the earth. We know where we stand. And if we haven't solid ground under us, how in creation can we ever hope to think anything through?

Professor William James, the father of applied psychology, has been dead for thirty-eight years. But if he were alive today, and could hear his formula for facing the worst, he would heartily approve it. How do I know that? Because he told his own students: "Be willing to have it so…. Be willing to have it so," he said, because "…Acceptance of what has happened is the first step in overcoming the consequences of any misfortune.'"

The same idea was expressed by Lin Yutang in his widely read book, *The Importance of Living*. "True peace of mind," said this Chinese philosopher, "comes from accepting the worst. Psychologically, I think, it means a release of energy."

Psychologically, it means a new release of energy! When we have accepted the worst, we have nothing more to lose. And that automatically means, we have everything to gain! "After facing the worst," Willis H. Carrier reported, "I immediately relaxed and felt a sense of peace that I hadn't experienced in days. From that time on, I was able to think."

Makes sense, doesn't it? Yet millions of people have wrecked their lives in angry turmoil, because they refused to accept the worst; refused to try to improve upon it; refused to salvage what they could from the wreck.

Here is one example, from a New York oil dealer who was a student in my class.

I was being blackmailed. I didn't believe it was possible. I never thought it could happen outside of the movies but I was actually being blackmailed! What happened was this: the oil company of which I was the head, had a number of delivery trucks and a number of drivers. At that time, OPA regulations were strictly in force, and we were rationed on the amount of oil we could deliver to any one of our customers. I didn't know it, but it seems that certain of our drivers had been delivering oil short to our regular customers, and then reselling the surplus to customers of their own.

The first inkling I had of these illegitimate transactions was when a man who claimed to be a government inspector came to see me one day and demanded hush money. He had got documentary proof of what our drivers had been doing, and he threatened to turn this proof over to the District Attorney's office if I didn't cough up.

I knew, of course, that I had nothing to worry about, personally at least. But I also knew that the law says a firm is responsible for the actions of its employees. What's more, I knew that if the case came to court, and it was aired in the newspapers, the bad publicity would ruin my business. And I was proud of my business – it had been founded by my father twenty-four years before.

I was so worried that I got sick. I didn't eat or sleep for three days and nights. I kept going around in crazy circles. Should I pay the money – five thousand dollars – or should I tell this man to go ahead and do his damnedest? Either way I tried to make up my mind, it ended up in a nightmare.

Then, on one Sunday night, I happened to pick up the booklet on How to Stop Worrying which I had been given in my Carnegie class in public speaking. I started to read it, and came across the story of Willis H. Carrier. 'Face the worst' it said. So I asked myself, 'What is the worst that can happen if I refuse to pay up, and these blackmailers turn their records over to the District Attorney?'

The answer was: 'the ruin of my business, that's the worst that can happen. I can't go to jail. All that can happen is that I shall be ruined by the publicity.'

I then said to myself, "All right, the business is ruined. I accept that mentally. What happens next?"

Well, with my business ruined, I would probably have to look for a job. That wasn't bad. I knew a lot about oil – there were several firms that might be glad to employ me.

I began to feel better. The blue funk I had been in for three days and nights began to lift a little. My emotions calmed down…And to my astonishment, I was able to think.

I was clear-headed enough now to face Step III- improve on the worst. As I thought of solutions, an entirely new angle presented itself to me. If I told my attorney the whole situation, he might find a way out which I hadn't thought of. I know it sounds stupid to say that this hadn't even occurred to me before – but, of course, I hadn't been thinking, I had only been worrying! I immediately made up my mind that I would see my attorney first thing in the morning – and then I went to bed and slept like a log.

How did it end? Well, the next morning my lawyer told me to go and see the District Attorney and tell him the truth. I did precisely that. When I finished I was astonished to hear the D.A. say that this blackmail racket had been going on for months and that the man who claimed to be a 'government agent' was a crook wanted by the police. What a relief to *hear all this after I had tormented myself for three days and nights wondering whether I should hand over five thousand dollars to this professional swindler!*

This experience taught me a lasting lesson. Now, whenever I face a pressing problem that threatens to worry me, I give it what I call 'the old Willis H. Carrier formula'.

At just about the same time Willis H. Carrier was worrying over the gas-cleaning equipment he was installing in a plant in Crystal City, Missouri, a chap from Broken Bow, Nebraska, was making out his will. His name was Earl P. Haney, and he had duodenal ulcers. Three doctors, including a celebrated ulcer specialist, had pronounced Mr. Haney an "incurable case". They had told him not to eat this or that, and not to worry or fret – to keep perfectly calm. They also told him to make out his will!

These ulcers had already forced Earl P. Haney to give up a fine and highly paid position. So now he had nothing to do, nothing to look forward to except a lingering death.

Then he made a decision: a rare and excellent one. "Since I have only a little while to live," he said, "I may as well make the most of it. I have always wanted to travel around the world before I die. If I am ever going to do it, I'll have to do it now." So he bought his ticket.

The doctors were appalled. "We must warn you," they said to Mr. Haney, "that if you do take this trip, you will be buried at sea."

"No, I won't," he replied. "I have promised my relatives that I will be buried in the family plot at Broken Row, Nebraska. So I am going to buy a casket and take it with me."

He purchased a casket, put it aboard ship, and then made arrangements with the steamship company in the event of his death, to put his corps in a freezing compartment and keep it there till the liner returned home. He set out on his trip.

"I drank highballs, and smoked long cigars on that trip," Mr. Haney says in a letter that I have before me now. *"I ate all kinds of food, even strange native foods which were guaranteed to kill me. I enjoyed myself more than I had in years. We ran into monsoons and typhoons which should have put me in my casket, if only from fright, but I got an enormous kick out of all this adventure.*

I played games aboard the ship, sang songs, made new friends and stayed up half the night. When we reached China and India, I realised that the business troubles and cares that I had faced back home were paradise compared to the poverty and hunger. I stopped all my senseless worrying. When I returned to America, I had gained ninety pounds. I had almost forgotten I had ever had a stomach ulcer. I had never felt better in my life. I promptly sold the casket back to the undertaker, and went back to business. I haven't been ill a day since.

So, the rule to follow is: If you have a worry problem, apply the magic formula of Willis H. Carrier by doing these three things:

A Magic Formula for Solving Worry Situations

1. Ask yourself, 'What is the worst that can possibly happen?'
2. Prepare to accept it if you have to.
3. Then calmly proceed to improve on the worst.

2

HOW TO ANALYSE AND
SOLVE WORRY PROBLEMS

Will the magic formula of Willis H. Carrier solve all worry problems? No, of course not. Then what is the answer? The answer is that we must equip ourselves to deal with different kinds of worries by learning the three basic steps of problem analysis. The three steps are:

1. Get the facts.
2. Analyse the facts.
3. Arrive at a decision – and then act on that decision.

Let's take the first rule: Get the facts.

Why is it so important to get the facts? Because unless we have the facts we can't possibly attempt to solve our problem intelligently. Without the facts, all we can do is stew around in confusion. My idea? No, that was the idea of the late Herbert E. Hawkes, Dean of Columbia College, Columbia University, for twenty-two years. He had helped two hundred thousand students solve their worry problems; and he told me that confusion is the chief cause of worry". He put it this way: "Half the worry in the world is caused by people trying to make decisions before they have sufficient knowledge on which to base a decision. For example," he said, "if I have a problem which has to be faced at three o'clock next Tuesday, I refuse even to try to make a decision about it until next Tuesday arrives. In the meantime, I concentrate on getting all the facts that bear on the problem. I don't worry," he said, "I don't agonize over my problem. I don't lose any sleep, I simply concentrate on getting the facts. And by the time Tuesday rolls around, if I've got all the facts, the problem usually solves itself!"

I asked Dean Hawkes if this meant he had licked worry entirely. "Yes," he said, "I think I can honestly say that my life is now almost totally devoid of worry. I have found," he went on, "that if a man will devote his time to securing facts in an impartial, objective way, his worries usually evaporate in the light of knowledge."

Let me repeat that: "If a man will devote his time, to securing facts in an impartial, objective way, his worries will usually evaporate in the light of knowledge."

But what do most of us do? If we bother with facts at all and Thomas Edison said in all seriousness, "There is no expedient to which a man will not resort to avoid the labour of thinking, if we bother with facts at all, we hunt like bird dogs after the facts that bolster up what we already think – and ignore all the others! We want only the facts that justify our acts – the facts that fit in conveniently with our wishful thinking and justify our preconceived prejudices!

As André Maurois put it: "Everything that is in agreement with our personal desires seems true. Everything that isn't, puts us into a rage."

Is it any wonder, then, that we find it so hard to get at the answers to our problems? Wouldn't we have the same trouble trying to solve a second-grade arithmetic problem, if we went ahead on the assumption that two plus two equals five? Yet there are a lot of people in this world who make life hell for themselves and others by insisting that two plus two equals five or maybe five hundred.

What can we do about it? We have to keep our emotions out of our thinking; and, as Dean Hawkes put it, we must secure the facts in "an impartial, objective" manner.

That is not an easy task when we are worried. When we are worried, our emotions are riding high. But here are two ideas that I have found helpful when trying to step aside from my problems, in order to see the facts in a clear, objective manner.

1. When trying to get the facts, I pretend that I am collecting this information not for myself, but for some other person. This helps me to take a cold, impartial view of the evidence. This helps me eliminate my emotions.

2. While trying to collect the facts about the problem that is worrying me, I sometimes pretend that I am a lawyer preparing to argue the other side of the issue. In other words, I try to get all the facts against myself – all the facts that are damaging to my wishes, all the facts I don't like to face.

Then I write down both, my side of the case and the other side of the case – and I generally find that the truth lies somewhere in between these two extremities.

Here is the point I am trying to make. Neither you nor I nor Einstein nor the Supreme Court of the United States is brilliant enough to reach an intelligent decision on any problem without first getting the facts. Thomas Edison knew that. At the time of his death, he had two thousand five hundred notebooks filled with facts about the problems he was facing.

So Rule 1 for solving our problems is: Get the facts. Let's do what Dean Hawkes did: let's not even attempt to solve our problems without first collecting all the facts in an impartial manner.

However, getting all the facts in the world won't do us any good until we analyse them and interpret them.

I have found from costly experience that it is much easier to analyse the facts after writing them down. In fact, merely writing the facts on a piece of paper and stating our problem clearly goes a long way towards helping us to reach a sensible decision. As Charles Kettering says: "A problem well stated is a problem half solved."

Let me show you all this as it works out in practice. Since the Chinese say one picture is worth ten thousand words, suppose I show you a picture of how one man put exactly what we are talking about into concrete action.

Let's take the case of Galen Litchfield – a man I have known for several years; one of the most successful American business men in the Far East. Mr. Litchfield was in China in 1942, when the Japanese invaded Shanghai. And here is his story as he told it to me while a guest in my home:

"Shortly after the Japs took Pearl Harbour," Galen Litchfield began, "they came swarming into Shanghai. I was the manager of the Asia Life Insurance Company in Shanghai. They sent us an 'army liquidator' – he was really an admiral and gave me orders to assist this man in liquidating our assets. I didn't have any choice in the matter. I could co-operate – or else. And the 'or else' was certain death.

"I went through the motions of doing what I was told, because I had no alternative. But there was one block of securities, worth $750,000, which I left off the list I gave to the admiral. I left that block of securities off the list because they belonged to our Hong Kong organization and had nothing to do with the Shanghai assets. All the same, I feared I might be in hot water if the Japs found out what I had done. And soon, they found out.

"I wasn't in the office when the discovery was made, but my head accountant was there. He told me that the Jap admiral flew into a rage, and stamped and swore, and called me a thief and a traitor! I had defied the Japanese army! I knew what that meant. I would be thrown into the Bridgehouse!

"The Bridgehouse! The torture chamber of the Japanese Gestapo! I had personal friends who chose to kill themselves rather than be taken to that prison. I also had other friends who had died in that place after ten days of questioning and torture. Now I was slated for the Bridgehouse myself!

"What did I do? I heard the news on Sunday afternoon. I suppose I should have been terrified. And I would have been terrified if I hadn't had a definite technique for solving my problems. For years, whenever I was worried I had always gone to my typewriter and written down two questions – and the answers to these questions."

1. What am I worrying about?
2. What can I do about it?

"I used to try to answer those questions without writing them down. But I stopped that years ago. I found that writing down both the questions and the answers clarifies my thinking.

So, that Sunday afternoon, I went directly to my room at the Shanghai Y.M.C.A., and got out my typewriter. I wrote:

I. What am I worrying about?
    I am afraid I will be thrown into the Bridgehouse tomorrow morning.
    Then I typed out the second question:

2.   What can I do about it?

I spent hours thinking out and writing down the four courses of action I could take – and what the probable consequence of each action would be:

A.   I can try to explain to the Japanese admiral. But he "no speak English." If I try to explain to him through an interpreter, I may stir him up again. That might mean death, for he is cruel, would rather dump me in the Bridgehouse than bother talking about it.

B.   I can try to escape. Impossible!. They keep track of me all the time. I have to check in and out of my room at the Y.M.C.A. If I try to escape, I'll probably be captured and shot.

C.   I can stay here in my room and not go near the office again. If I do, the Japanese admiral will be suspicious, will probably send soldiers to get me and throw me into the Bridgehouse without giving me a chance to say a word.

D.   I can go down to the office as usual on Monday morning. If I do, there is a chance that the Japanese admiral may be so busy that he will not think of what I did. Even if he does think of it, he may have cooled off and may not bother me. If this happens, I am all right. Even if he does bother me. I'll still have a chance to try to explain to him. So, going down to the office as usual on Monday morning, and acting as if nothing had gone wrong gives me two chances to escape the Bridgehouse.

"As soon as I thought it all out and decided to accept the fourth plan – to go down to the office as usual on Monday morning, I felt immensely relieved.

"When I entered the office the next morning, the Japanese admiral sat there with a cigarette dangling from his mouth. He glared at me as he always did; and said nothing. Six weeks later, thank God, he went back to Tokyo and my worries ended.

"As I have already said, I probably saved my life by sitting down that Sunday afternoon and writing out all the various steps I could take and then writing down the probable consequence of each step and calmly coming to a decision. If I hadn't done that, I might have floundered and hesitated and done the wrong thing on the spur of the moment. If I hadn't thought out my problem and come to a decision, I would have been frantic with worry all Sunday afternoon. I wouldn't have slept that night. I would have gone down to the office Monday morning with a harassed and worried look; and that alone might have aroused the suspicion of the Japanese admiral and spurred him to act.

"Experience has proved to me, the enormous value of arriving at a decision. It is the failure to arrive at a fixed purpose, the inability to stop going round and round in maddening circles that drives men to nervous breakdowns and living hells. I find that fifty percent of my worries vanish once I arrive at a clear, definite decision; and another forty percent usually vanishes once I start to carry out that decision,

"So I banish about ninety percent of my worries by taking these four steps:

1. Writing down precisely what I am worrying about.
2. Writing down what I can do about it.
3. Deciding what to do.
4. Starting immediately to carry out that decision."

Galen Litchfield is now the Far Eastern Director for Starr, Park and Freeman, Inc., in John Street, New York, representing large insurance and financial interests.

In fact, as I said before, Galen Litchfield today is one of the most important American businessmen in Asia; and he confessed to me that he owes a large part of his success to this method of analysing worry and meeting it head-on.

Why is his method so superb? Because it is efficient, concrete, and goes directly to the heart of the problem. On top of all that, it is climaxed by the third and indispensable rule: Do something about it. Unless we carry out our action, all our fact-finding and analysis is whistling upwind – it's a sheer waste of energy. William James said this: "When once a decision is reached and execution is the order of the day, dismiss absolutely all responsibility and care about the outcome." In this case, William James undoubtedly used the word "care" as a synonym for "anxiety". He meant, once you have made a careful decision based on facts, go into action. Don't stop to reconsider. Don't hesitate, worry and retrace your steps. Don't lose yourself in self-doubting which begets other doubts. Don't keep looking back over your shoulder.

I once asked Waite Phillips, one of Oklahoma's most prominent oil men, how he carried out decisions. He replied: "I find that to keep thinking about our problems beyond a certain point is bound to create confusion and worry. There comes a time when any more investigation and thinking are harmful. There comes a time when we must decide and act and never look back."

Why don't you employ Galen Litchfield's technique to one of your worries right now?

Here is:

Question No.1- What am I worrying about?

_____

_____

_____

_____

_____

_____

_____

Question No. 2- What can I do about it?

_____

_____

_____

_____

_____

_____

_____

Question No.3 Here is what 1 am going to do about it.

_____

_____

_____

_____

_____

_____

Question No. 4 When am I going to start doing it?

_____

_____

_____

_____

_____

_____

_____

3

DON'T TRY TO SAW SAWDUST

As I write this sentence, I can look out of my window and see some dinosaur tracks in my garden – dinosaur tracks embedded in shale and stone. I purchased those dinosaur tracks from the Peabody Museum of Yale University; and I have a letter from the curator of the Peabody Museum, saying that those tracks were made 180 million years ago. Even a Mongolian idiot wouldn't dream of trying to go back 180 million years to change those tracks. Yet, that would not be any more foolish than worrying because we can't go back and change what happened 180 seconds ago – and a lot of us are doing just that. To be sure, we may do something to modify the effects of what happened 180 seconds ago but we can't possibly change the event that occurred then.

There is only one way on god's green footstool that the past can be constructive, and that is by calmly analysing our mistakes and profiting from them and forgetting them.

I know that is true but have I always had the courage and sense to do it? To answer that question, let me tell you about a fantastic experience I had years ago. I let more than three hundred thousand dollars slip through my fingers without making a penny's profit. It happened like this: I launched a large-scale enterprise in adult education, opened branches in various cities, and spent money lavishly on overhead and advertising. I was so busy with teaching that I had neither the time nor the desire to look after finances. I was too naive to realise that I needed an astute business manager to watch expenses.

Finally, after about a year, I discovered a sobering and shocking truth. I discovered that despite our enormous intake, we had not netted any profit whatever. After discovering that, I should have done two things: First, I should have had the sense to do what George Washington Carver, the negro scientist, did when he lost forty thousand dollars in a bank crash – the savings of a lifetime. When someone asked him if he knew he was bankrupt, he replied, "Yes, I heard" – and went on with his teaching. He wiped the loss out of his mind so completely that he never mentioned it again.

Here is the second thing I should have done: I should have analysed my mistakes and learned a lasting lesson.

But frankly, I didn't do either one of these things. Instead, I went into a tailspin of worry. For months I was in a daze. I lost sleep and I lost weight. Instead of learning a lesson from this enormous mistake, I went right ahead and did the same thing again on a smaller scale!

It is embarrassing for me to admit all this stupidity, but I discovered long ago that "it is easier to teach twenty what were good to be done than to be one of twenty to follow mine own teaching."

Some readers are going to snort at the idea of making so much over a hackneyed proverb like "Don't cry over spilt milk" I know it is trite, commonplace, and a platitude. I know you have heard it a thousand times. But I also know that these hackneyed proverbs contain the very essence of the distilled wisdom of all ages. They have come out of the fiery experience of the human race and have been handed down through countless generations. If you were to read everything that has ever been written about worry by the great scholars of all time, you would never read anything more basic or more profound than such hackneyed proverbs as "Don't cross your bridges until you come to them" and "Don't cry over spilt milk". If we only applied those two proverbs – instead of snorting at them – we wouldn't need this book at all. In fact, if we applied most of the old proverbs, we would lead almost perfect lives. However, knowledge isn't power until it is applied; and the purpose of this book is not to tell you something new. The purpose of this book is to remind you of what you already know and to kick you in the shins and inspire you to do something about applying it.

So let's remember:

Don't try to saw sawdust.

4

IF YOU HAVE A LEMON,
MAKE A LEMONADE

While writing this book, I dropped in one day at the University of Chicago and asked the Chancellor, Robert Maynard Hutchins, how he kept from worrying. He replied, "I have always tried to follow a bit of advice given me by the late Julius Rosenwald, President of Sears, Roebuck and Company: 'When you have a lemon, make lemonade.'"

That is what a great educator does. But the fool does the exact opposite. If he finds that life has handed him a lemon, he gives up and says, 'Tin beaten. It is fate. I haven't got a chance.' Then he proceeds to rail against the world and indulge in an orgy of self-pity. But when the wise man is handed a lemon, he says: "What lesson can I learn from this misfortune? How can I improve my situation? How can I turn this lemon into a lemonade?"

After spending a lifetime studying people and their hidden reserves of power, the great psychologist, Alfred Adler, declared that one of the wonder-filled characteristics of human beings is "their power to turn a minus into a plus."

Here is an interesting and stimulating story of a woman I know who did just that. Her name is Thelma Thompson.

During the war, my husband was stationed at an Army training camp near the Mojave Desert, in New Mexico. I went to live there in order to be near him. I hated the place. I loathed it. I had never before been so miserable. My husband was ordered out on manoeuvres in the Mojave Desert, and I was left in a tiny shack alone. The heat was unbearable – 125 degrees in the shade of a cactus. Not a soul to talk to but Mexicans and Indians, and they couldn't speak English. The wind blew incessantly, and both, the food I ate and the very air I breathed, were filled with sand, sand, and sand! "I was so utterly wretched, so sorry for myself that I wrote to my parents. 1 told them I was giving up and coming back home. I said I couldn't stand it one minute longer. I would rather be in jail. My father answered my letter with just two lines – two lines that will always sing in my memory – two lines that completely altered my life

Two men looked out from prison bars.
One saw the mud, the other saw stairs.

I read those two lines over and over. I was ashamed of myself. I made up my mind I would find out what was good in my present situation. I would look for the stars.

I made friends with the natives, and their reaction amazed me. When I showed interest in their weaving and pottery, they gave me presents of their favourite pieces which they had refused to sell to tourists. I studied the fascinating forms of the cactus and the yuccas and the Joshua trees. I learned about prairie dogs, watched for the desert sunsets, and hunted for seashells that had been left there millions of years ago when the sands of the desert had been an ocean floor.

What brought about this astonishing change in me? The Mojave Desert hadn't changed. The Indians hadn't changed. But I had. I had changed my attitude of mind. And by doing so, I transformed a wretched experience into the most exciting adventure of my life. I was stimulated and excited by this new world that I had discovered. I was so excited I wrote a book about it – a novel that was published under the title Bright Ramparts. I had looked out of my self-created prison and found the stars.

Thelma Thompson, you discovered an old truth that the Greeks taught five hundred years before Christ was born: "The best things are the most difficult."

Harry Emerson Fosdick repeated it again in the twentieth century: "Happiness is not mostly pleasure; it is mostly victory."

Yes, the victory that comes from a sense of achievement, of triumph, of turning our lemons into lemonades.

I once visited a happy fanner down in Florida who turned even a poison lemon into lemonade. When he first got this farm, he was discouraged. The land was so wretched he could neither grow fruit nor raise pigs. Nothing thrived there but scrub oaks and rattlesnakes. Then he got his idea. He would turn his liability into an asset: he would make the most of these rattlesnakes. To everyone's amazement, he started canning rattlesnake meat. When I stopped to visit him a few years ago, I found that tourists were pouring in to see his rattlesnake farm at the rate of twenty thousand a year. His business was thriving. I saw poison from the fangs of his rattlers being shipped to laboratories to make anti-venom toxin. I saw rattlesnake skins being sold at fancy prices to make women's shoes and handbags. I saw canned rattlesnake meat being shipped to customers all over the world. I bought a picture postcard of the place and mailed it at the local post office of the village, which had been re-christened "Rattlesnake, Florida", in honour of a man who had turned a poison lemon into sweet lemonade.

As I have travelled up and down and back and forth across America time after time, it has been my privilege to meet dozens of men and women who have demonstrated "their power to turn a minus into a plus."

The late William Bolitho, author of *Twelve Against the Gods*, put it like this: "The most important thing in life is not to capitalise on your gains. Any fool can do that. The most important thing is to profit from your losses. That requires intelligence; and it makes the difference between a man of sense and a fool."

Bolitho uttered those words after he had lost a leg in a railway accident. But I know a man who lost both legs and turned his minus into a plus. His name is Ben Fortson. I met him in a hotel elevator in Atlanta, Georgia. As I stepped into the elevator, I noticed this cheerful-looking man, who had both legs missing, sitting in a wheelchair in a comer of the elevator. When the elevator stopped at his floor, he asked me pleasantly if I would step to one comer, so he could manage his chair better, "So sorry," he said, "to inconvenience you" – and a deep, heart-warming smile lighted his face as he said it.

When I left the elevator and went to my room, I could think of nothing but this cheerful boy. So I hunted him up and asked him to tell me his story.

"It happened in 1929," he told me with a smile. "I had gone out to cut a load of hickory poles to stake the beans in my garden. I had loaded the poles on my Ford and started back home. Suddenly one pole slipped under the car and jammed the steering apparatus at the very moment I was making a sharp turn. The car shot over an embankment and hurled me against a tree. My spine was hurt. My legs were paralysed.

"I was twenty-four when that happened, and I have never taken a step since."

Twenty-four years old and sentenced to a wheelchair for the rest of his life! I asked him how he managed to take it so courageously, and he said, "I didn't." He said he raged and rebelled. He fumed about his fate. But as the years dragged on, he found that his rebellion wasn't getting him anything except bitterness. "I finally realised," he said, "that other people were kind and courteous to me. So the least I could do was to be kind and courteous to them."

I asked if he still felt, after all these years, that his accident had been a terrible misfortune, and he promptly said, "No." He said, "I'm almost glad now that it happened." He told me that after he got over the shock and resentment, he began to live in a different world. He began to read and developed a love for good literature. In fourteen years, he said, he had read at least fourteen hundred books and those books had opened up new horizons for him and made his life richer than he ever thought possible. He began to listen to good music, and he is now thrilled by great symphonies that would have bored him before. But the biggest change was that he had time to think. "For the first time in my life," he said, "I was able to look at the world and get a real sense of values. I began to realise that most of the things I had been striving for before weren't worthwhile at all."

As a result of his reading, he became interested in politics, studied public questions, made speeches from his wheel-chair! He got to know people and people got to know him. Today Ben Fortson, still in his wheel-chair, is Secretary of State for the State of Georgia!

During the last thirty-five years, I have been conducting adult-education classes in New York City, and I have discovered that one of the major regrets of many adults is that they never went to college. They seem to think that not having a college education is a great handicap. I know that this isn't necessarily true because I have known thousands of successful men who never went beyond high school. So I often tell these students the story of a man I knew who had never finished even grade school. He was brought up in blighting poverty. When his father died, his father's friends had to chip in to pay for the coffin in which he was buried. After his father's death, his mother worked in an umbrella factory ten hours a day and brought piecework home and worked until eleven o'clock at night.

The boy brought up in these circumstances went in for amateur dramatics put on by a club in his church. He got such a thrill out of acting that he decided to take up public speaking. This led him into politics. By the time he reached thirty, he was elected to the New York State legislature. But he was woefully unprepared for such a responsibility. In fact, he told me that frankly, he didn't know what it was all about. He studied the long, complicated bills that he was supposed to vote on – but, as far as he was concerned, those bills might as well have been written in the language of the Choctaw Indians. He was worried and bewildered when he was made a member of the committee on forests before he had ever set foot in a forest. He was worried and bewildered when he was made a member of the State Banking Commission before he had ever had a bank account. He told me that he was so discouraged that he would have resigned from the legislature if he hadn't been ashamed to admit defeat to his mother. In despair, he decided to study sixteen hours a day and turn his lemon of ignorance into a lemonade of knowledge. By doing that, he transformed himself from a local politician into a national figure and made himself so outstanding that *The New York Times* called him "the best-loved citizen of New York."

I am talking about Al Smith.

Ten years after Al Smith set out on his programme of political self-education, he was the greatest living authority on the government of New York State. He was elected Governor of New York for four terms – a record never attained by any other man till then. In 1928, he was the Democratic candidate for President. Six great universities – including Columbia and Harvard – conferred honorary degrees upon this man who had never gone beyond grade school.

Al Smith himself told me that none of these things would ever have come to pass if he hadn't worked hard, sixteen hours a day, to turn his minus into a plus.

Nietzche's formula for the superior man was "not only to bear up under necessity but to love it."

The more I have studied the careers of men of achievement, the more deeply I have been convinced that a surprisingly large number of them succeeded because they started out with handicaps that spurred them on to great endeavour and great rewards. As William James said: "Our infirmities help us unexpectedly."

Yes, it is highly probable that Milton wrote better poetry because he was blind and that Beethoven composed better music because he was deaf.

Suppose we are so discouraged that we feel there is no hope of our ever being able to turn our lemons into lemonade – then here are two reasons why we ought to try, anyway – two reasons why we have everything to gain and nothing to lose.

Reason one: We may succeed.

Reason two: Even if we don't succeed, the mere attempt to turn our minus into a plus will cause us to look forward instead of backward; it will replace negative thoughts with positive thoughts; it will release creative energy and spur us to get so busy that we won't have either the time or the inclination to mourn over what is past and for ever gone.

So, to cultivate a mental attitude that will bring us peace and happiness, let's do this:

When fate hands us a lemon, let's try to make a lemonade.

5

DO THIS – AND CRITICISM CAN'T HURT YOU

I once interviewed Major-General Smedley Butler – old "Gimlet-Eye". Old "Hell-Devil" Butler! Remember him? The most colourful, swash buckling general to ever command the United States Marines.

He told me that when he was young, he was desperately eager to be popular, wanted to make a good impression on everyone. In those days the slightest criticism smarted and stung. But he confessed that thirty years in the Marines had toughened his hide. "I have been berated and insulted," he said, "and denounced as a yellow dog, a snake, and a skunk. I have been cursed by the experts. I have been called every possible combination of unprintable cuss words in the English language. Bother me? Huh! When I hear someone cussing me now, I never turn my head to see who is talking."

Maybe old "Gimlet-Eye" Butler was too indifferent to criticism, but one thing is sure: most of us take the little jibes and javelins that are hurled at us far too seriously. I remember the time, years ago when a reporter from the New York Sun attended a demonstration meeting of my adult-education classes and lampooned me and my work. Was I burned up? I took it as a personal insult. I telephoned Gil Hodges, the Chairman of the Executive Committee of the Sun, and practically demanded that he print an article stating the facts – instead of ridicule. I was determined to make the punishment fit the crime.

I am ashamed now of the way I acted. I realise now that half the people who bought the paper never saw that article. Half of those who read it regarded it as a source of innocent merriment. Half of those who gloated over it forgot all about it in a few weeks, I realise now that people are not thinking about you and me or caring what is said about us. They are thinking about themselves – before breakfast, after breakfast, and right on until ten minutes past midnight. They would be a thousand times more concerned about a slight headache of their own than they would about the news of your death or mine.

Even if you and I are lied about, ridiculed, double-crossed, knifed in the back, and sold down the river by one out of every six of our most intimate friends – let's not indulge in an orgy of self-pity. Instead, let's remind ourselves that that's precisely what happened to Jesus. One of His twelve most intimate friends turned traitor for a bribe that would amount, in our modem money, to about nineteen dollars. Another one of His twelve most intimate friends openly deserted Jesus the moment He got into trouble, and declared three times that he didn't even know Jesus. One out of six! That is what happened to Jesus. Why should you and I expect a better score?

I discovered years ago that although I couldn't keep people from criticising me unjustly, I could do something infinitely more important: I could determine whether I would let the unjust condemnation disturb me.

Let's be clear about this: I am not advocating ignoring all criticism. Far from it. I am talking about ignoring only unjust criticism. I once asked Eleanor Roosevelt how she handled unjust criticism – and god knows she's had a lot of it. She probably has more ardent friends and more violent enemies than any other woman who ever lived in the White House.

She told me that as a young girl she was almost morbidly shy, afraid of what people might say. She was so afraid of criticism that one day she asked her aunt, Theodore Roosevelt's sister, for advice. She said: "Auntie Bye, I want to do so-and-so. But I'm afraid of being criticised."

Teddy Roosevelt's sister looked her in the eye and said: "Never be bothered by what people say, as long as you know in your heart you are right." Eleanor Roosevelt told me that that bit of advice proved to be her Rock of Gibraltar years later, when she was in the White House. She told me that the only way we can avoid all criticism is to be like a Dresden-china figure and stay on a shelf.

"Do what you feel in your heart to be right – for you'll be criticised anyway. You'll be damned if you do, and damned if you don't." That is her advice.

When the late Matthew C. Brush was president of the American International Corporation at 40 Wall Street, I asked him if he was ever sensitive to criticism; and he replied, "Yes, I was very sensitive to it in my early days. I was eager then to have all the employees in the organisation think I was perfect. If they didn't, it worried me. I would try to please first one person who had been sounding off against me; but the very thing I did to patch it up with him would make someone else mad. Then when I tried to fix it up with this person, I would stir up a couple of other bumblebees. I finally discovered that the more I tried to pacify and to smooth over injured feelings in order to escape personal criticism, the more certain I was to increase my enemies. So finally I said to myself, if you get your head above the crowd, you're going to be criticised. So get used to the idea. That helped me tremendously. From that time on I made it a rule to do the very best I could and then put up my old umbrella and let the rain of criticism drain off me instead of running down my neck."

Deems Taylor went a bit further: he let the rain of criticism run down his neck and had a good laugh over it – in public. When he was giving his comments during the intermission of the Sunday afternoon radio concerts of the New York Phil-harmonic-Symphony Orchestra, one woman wrote him a letter calling him "a liar, a traitor, a snake and a moron".

On the following week's broadcast, Mr. Taylor read this letter over the radio to millions of listeners. In his book, *Of Men & Music*, he tells us that a few days later he received another letter from the same lady, "expressing her unaltered opinion that I was still a liar, a traitor, a snake and a moron. I have a suspicion," adds Mr. Taylor, "that she didn't care for that talk." We can't keep from admiring a man who takes criticism like that. We admire his serenity, his unshaken poise, and his sense of humour.

When Charles Schwab was addressing the student body at Princeton, he confessed that one of the most important lessons he had ever learned was taught to him by an old German who worked in Schwab's steel mill. This old German got involved in a hot wartime argument with the other steelworkers, and they tossed him into the river. "When he came into my office," Mr. Schwab said, "covered with mud and water, I asked him what he had said to the men who had thrown him into the river, and he replied: "I just laughed." Mr. Schwab declared that he had adopted that old German's words as his motto "Just laugh." That motto is especially good when you are the victim of unjust criticism. You can answer the man who answers you back, but what can you say to the man who "just laughs"?

Lincoln might have broken under the strain of the Civil War if he hadn't learned the folly of trying to answer all his savage critics. He finally said: "If I were to try to read, much less to answer, all the attacks made on me, this shop might as well be closed for any other business. I do the very best I know how the very best I can;

and I mean to keep on doing so until the end. If the end brings me out all right, then what is said against me won't matter. If the end brings me out wrong, then ten angels swearing I was right would make no difference."

When you and I are unjustly criticised, let's remember:

Do the very best you can: and then put up your old umbrella and keep the rain of criticism from running down the back of your neck.

How to Add One Hour a Day to Your Waking Life

Why am I writing a chapter on preventing fatigue in a book on preventing worry? That is simple: because fatigue often produces worry, or, at least, it makes you susceptible to worry. Any medical student will tell you that fatigue lowers physical resistance to the common cold and hundreds of other diseases and any psychiatrist will tell you that fatigue also lowers your resistance to the emotions of fear and worry. So preventing fatigue tends to prevent worry.

Did I say "tends to prevent worry"? That is putting it mildly. Dr. Edmund Jacobson goes much further. Dr. Jacobson has written two books on relaxation: *Progressive Relaxation* and *You Must Relax;* and as director of the University of Chicago Laboratory for Clinical Physiology, he has spent years conducting investigations in using relaxation as a method in medical practice. He declares that any nervous or emotional state "fails to exist in the presence of complete relaxation". That is another way of saying: You cannot continue to worry if you relax.

So, to prevent fatigue and worry, the first rule is: Rest often. Rest before you get tired.

Why is that so important? Because fatigue accumulates with astonishing rapidity. The United States Army has discovered by repeated tests that even young men – men toughened by years of Army training – can march better, and hold up longer, if they throw down their packs and rest ten minutes out of every hour. So the Army forces them to do just that. Your heart is just as smart as the U.S. Army. Your heart pumps enough blood through your body every day to fill a railway tank car. It exerts enough energy every twenty-four hours to shovel twenty tons of coal onto a platform three feet high. It does this incredible amount of work for fifty, seventy, or maybe ninety years. How can it stand it? Dr. Walter B. Cannon, of the Harvard Medical School, explains it. He says 'Most people have the idea that the heart is working all the time. As a matter of fact, there is a definite rest period after each contraction. When beating at a moderate rate of seventy pulses per minute, the heart is actually working only nine hours out of the twenty-four. In the aggregate, its rest periods total a full fifteen hours per day.'

During World War II, Winston Churchill, in his late sixties and early seventies, was able to work sixteen hours a day, year after year, directing the war efforts of the British Empire. A phenomenal record. His secret? He worked in bed each morning until eleven o'clock, reading papers, dictating orders, making telephone calls, and holding important conferences. After lunch, he went to bed once more and slept for an hour. In the evening he went to bed once more and slept for two hours before having dinner at eight. He didn't cure fatigue. He didn't have to cure it. He prevented it. Because he rested frequently, he was able to work on, fresh and fit, until long past midnight.

When I asked Eleanor Roosevelt how she was able to carry such an exhausting schedule during the twelve years she was in the White House, she said that before meeting a crowd or making a speech, she would often sit in a chair or davenport, close her eyes, and relax for twenty minutes.

A physical worker can do more work if he takes more time out for rest. Frederick Taylor demonstrated that while working as a scientific management engineer with the Bethlehem Steel Company, he observed that labouring men were loading approximately 12 tons of pig-iron per man each day on freight cars and that they were exhausted at noon. He made a scientific study of all the fatigue factors involved, and declared that these' men should be loading not 12 tons of pig-iron per day, but forty-seven tons per day! He figured that they ought to do almost four times as much as they were doing, and not be exhausted. But to prove it, Taylor selected a Mr. Schmidt who was required to work by the stop-watch. Schmidt was told by the man who stood over him with a watch, "Now pick up a 'pig' and walk.... Now sit down and rest..., Now walk... Now rest,"

What happened? Schmidt carried forty-seven tons of pig iron each day while the other men carried only 12 tons per man. And he practically never failed to work at this pace during the three years that Frederick Taylor was at Bethlehem. Schmidt was able to do this because he rested before he got tired. He worked approximately 26 minutes out of the hour and rested 34 minutes. He rested more than he worked – yet he did almost four times as much work as the others! Is this mere hearsay? No, you can read the record yourself in Principles Scientific Management by Frederick Winslow Taylor. Let me repeat: do what the Army does – take frequent rests. Do what your heart does – rest before you get tired, and you will add one hour a day to your waking life.

6

WHAT MAKES YOU TIRED – AND WHAT YOU CAN DO ABOUT IT

Here is an astounding and significant fact: Mental work alone can't make you tired. Sounds absurd, right? But a few years ago, scientists tried to find out how long the human brain could labour without reaching "a diminished capacity for work", the scientific definition of fatigue. To the amazement of these scientists, they discovered that blood passing through the brain, when it is active, shows no fatigue at all! If you took blood from the veins of a day labourer while he was working, you would find it full of "fatigue toxins" and fatigue products. But if you took a drop of blood from the brain of an Albert Einstein, it would show no fatigue toxins whatever at the end of the day.

So far as the brain is concerned, it can work "as well and as swiftly at the end of eight or even twelve hours of effort as at the beginning." The brain is utterly tireless.... So what makes you tired?

Psychiatrists declare that most of our fatigue derives from our mental and emotional attitudes. One of England's most distinguished psychiatrists, J. A. Hadfield, says in his book *The Psychology of Power,* "the greater part of the fatigue from which we suffer is of mental origin; in fact exhaustion of purely physical origin is rare."

One of America's most distinguished psychiatrists, Dr. A. A. Brill, goes even further. He declares, "One hundred percent of the fatigue of the sedentary worker in good health is due to psychological factors, by which we mean emotional factors."

What kinds of emotional factors tire the sedentary (or sitting) worker? Joy? Contentment? No! Never! Boredom, resentment, a feeling of not being appreciated, a feeling of futility, hurry, anxiety, worry – those are the emotional factors that exhaust the sitting worker, make him susceptible to colds, reduce his output, and send him home with a nervous headache. Yes, we get tired because our emotions produce nervous tensions in the body.

The Metropolitan Life Insurance Company pointed that out in a leaflet on fatigue: "Hard work by itself," says this great life-insurance company, "seldom causes fatigue which cannot be cured by a good sleep or rest.... Worry, tenseness, and emotional upsets are three of the biggest causes of fatigue. Often they are to blame when physical or mental work seems to be the cause.... Remember that a tense muscle is a working muscle. Ease up and save energy for important duties."

Stop now, right where you are, and give yourself a check-up! As you read these lines, are you scowling at the book? Do you feel a strain between the eyes? Are you sitting relaxed in your chair? Or are you hunching up your shoulders? Are the muscles of your face tense? Unless your entire body is as limp and relaxed as an old rag doll, you are at this very moment producing nervous tensions and muscular tensions. You are producing nervous tensions and nervous fatigue!

Why do we produce these unnecessary tensions in doing mental work? Josselyn says: "I find that the chief obstacle ... is the almost universal belief that hard work requires a feeling of effort, else it is not well done." So we scowl when we concentrate. We hunch up our shoulders. We call on our muscles to make the motion of effort, which in no way assists our brain in its work.

Here is an astonishing and tragic truth: millions of people who wouldn't dream of wasting dollars go right on wasting and squandering their energy with the recklessness of seven drunken sailors in Singapore.

What is the answer to this nervous fatigue? Relax! Relax! Relax! Learn to relax while you are doing your work!

Easy? No. You will probably have to reverse the habits of a lifetime. But it is worth the effort, for it may revolutionise your life! William James said, in his essay *The Gospel of Relaxation*: "The American over-tension and jerkiness and breathlessness and intensity and agony of expression ... are bad habits, nothing more or less." Tension is a habit. Relaxing is a habit. And bad habits can be broken, good habits formed.

How do you relax? Do you start with your mind, or do you start with your nerves? You don't start with either. You always begin to relax with your muscles!

Let's give it a try. To show how it is done, suppose we start with your eyes. Read this paragraph through, and when you've reached the end, lean back, close your eyes, and say to your eyes silently, "Let go. Let go. Stop straining, stop frowning. Let go. Let go." Repeat that over and over very slowly for a minute….

Didn't you notice that after a few seconds the muscles of the eyes began to obey? Didn't you feel as though some hand had wiped away the tension? Well, incredible as it seems, you have sampled in that one minute the whole key and secret to the art of relaxing. You can do the same thing with the jaw, with the muscles of the face, with the neck, with the shoulders, the whole of the body. But the most important organ of all is the eye. Dr. Edmund Jacobson of the University of Chicago has gone so far as to say that if you can completely relax the muscles of the eyes, you can forget all your trembles! The reason the eyes are so important in relieving nervous tension is that they burn up one-fourth of all the nervous energies consumed by the body. That is also why so many people with perfectly sound vision suffer from "eyestrain". They are tensing the eyes.

Here are five suggestions that will help you learn to relax:

1. Read a good book written on this subject.

2. Relax in odd moments. Let your body go limp like an old sock. I keep an old, maroon-coloured sock on my desk as I work – keep it there as a reminder of how limp I ought to be. If you haven't got a sock, a cat will do. Did you ever pick up a kitten sleeping in the sunshine? If so, both ends sagged like a wet newspaper. Even the yogis in India say that if you want to master the art of relaxation, study the cat. I never saw a tired cat, a cat with a nervous breakdown, or a cat suffering from insomnia, worry, or stomach ulcers. You will probably avoid these disasters if you learn to relax as the cat does.

3. Work, as much as possible, in a comfortable position Remember that tensions on the body produce aching shoulders and nervous fatigue.

4. Check yourself four or five times a day, and say to yourself, "Am I making my work harder than it actually is? Am I using muscles that have nothing to do with the work I am doing?" This will help you form the habit of relaxing, and as Dr. David Harold Fink says, "Among those who know psychology best, it is habits two to one."

5. Test yourself again at the end of the day, by asking yourself, "Just how tired am I? If I am tired, it is not because of the mental work I have done but because of the way I have done it." "I measure my accomplishments," says Daniel W. Josselyn, "not by how tired I am at the end of the day, but how tired I am not." He says, "When I feel particularly tired at the end of the day, or when irritability proves that my nerves are tired, I

know beyond question that it has been an inefficient day both as to quantity and quality." If every businessman would learn that same lesson, the death rate from "hypertension" would drop overnight. And we would stop filling up our sanatoriums and asylums with men who have been broken by fatigue and worry.

7

FOUR GOOD WORKING HABITS THAT WILL HELP PREVENT FATIGUE AND WORRY

Good Working Habit No. 1: Clear Your Desk of All Papers Except Those Relating to the Immediate Problem at Hand.

Roland L. Williams, President of Chicago and North-western Railway, says, "A person with his desk piled high with papers on various matters will find his work much easier and more accurate if he clears that desk of all but the immediate problem on hand. I call this good housekeeping, and it is the number-one step towards efficiency."

If you visit the Library of Congress in Washington, D.C., you will find five words painted on the ceiling – five words written by the poet Pope

"Order is Heaven's first law."

Order ought to be the first law of business, too. But is it? No, the average businessman's desk is cluttered up with papers that he hasn't looked at for weeks. In fact, the publisher of a New Orleans newspaper once told me that his secretary cleared up one of his desks and found a typewriter that had been missing for two years!

The mere sight of a desk littered with unanswered mail and reports and memos is enough to breed confusion, tension, and worries. It is much worse than that. The constant reminder of "a million things to do and no time to do them" can worry you not only into tension and fatigue, but it can also worry you into high blood pressure, heart trouble, and stomach ulcers.

But how can such an elementary procedure as clearing your desk and making decisions help you avoid this high pressure, this sense of must, this sense of an "unending stretch of things ahead that simply have to be done"? Dr. William L. Sadler, the famous psychiatrist, tells of a patient who, by using this simple device, avoided a nervous breakdown. The man was an executive in a big Chicago firm. When he came to Dr. Sadler's office, he was tense, nervous, worried. He knew he was heading for a tailspin, but he couldn't quit work. He had to have help. "While this man was telling me his story," Dr. Sadler says, "my telephone rang. It was the hospital calling; and, instead of deferring the matter, I took time right then to come to a decision. I always settle questions, if possible, right on the spot. I had no sooner hung up than the phone rang again. Again an urgent matter, which I took time to discuss. The third interruption came when a colleague of mine came to my office for advice on a patient who was critically ill. When I had finished with him, I turned to my caller and began to apologize for keeping him waiting. But he had brightened up. He had a completely different look on his face."

"Don't apologize, doctor!," this man said to Sadler. "In the last ten minutes, I think I've got a hunch as to what is wrong with me. I'm going back to my office and revise my working habits. But before I go, do you mind if I take a look inside your desk? Dr. Sadler opened up the drawers of his desk. All empty except for supplies. "Tell me," said the patient, "where do you keep your unfinished business? "Finished!" said Sadler.

"And where do you keep your unanswered mail?"

"Answered!" Sadler told him. "My rule is never to lay down a letter until I have answered it. I dictate the reply to my secretary at once."

Six weeks later, this same executive invited Dr. Sadler to come to his office. He was changed – and so was his desk. He opened the desk drawers to show there was no unfinished business inside of the desk. "Six weeks ago," this executive said, "I had three different desks in two different offices and was snowed under by my work. I was never finished. After talking to you, I came back here and cleared out a wagon-load of reports and old papers. Now I work at one desk, settle things as they come up, and don't have a mountain of unfinished business nagging at me and making me tense and worried. But the most astonishing thing is I've recovered completely. There is nothing wrong anymore with my health.

Good Working Habit No. 2: Do Things in the Order of Their Importance.

Henry L. Dougherty, founder of the nation-wide Cities Service Company, said that regardless of how much salary he paid, there were two abilities he found it almost impossible to find.

Those two priceless abilities are: first, the ability to think. Second, the ability to do things in the order of their importance.

Charles Luckman, the lad who started from scratch and climbed in twelve years to president of the Pepsodent Company, got a salary of a hundred thousand dollars a year, and made a million dollars besides – that lad declares that he owes much of his success to developing the two abilities that Henry L. Dougherty said he found almost impossible to find. Charles Luckman said: "As far back as I can remember, I have got up at five o'clock in the morning because I can think better then than any other time – I can think better then and plan my day, plan to do things in the order of their importance."

I know from long experience that one is not always able to do things in the order of their importance, but I also know that some kind of plan to do first things first is infinitely better than extemporising as you go along.

If George Bernard Shaw had not made it a rigid rule to do first things first, he would probably have failed as a writer and might have remained a bank cashier all his life. His plan called for writing five pages each day. That plan and his dogged determination to carry it through saved him. That plan inspired him to go right on writing five pages a day for nine heartbreaking years, even though he made a total of only thirty dollars in those nine years – about a penny a day.

Good Working Habit No. 3: When You Face a Problem, Solve It Then and There if You Have the Facts Necessary to Make a Decision Don't Keep Putting off Decisions.

One of my former students, the late H. P. Howell, told me that when he was a member of the board of directors of U.S. Steel, the meetings of the board were often long-drawn-out affairs – many problems were discussed, few decisions were made. The result: each member of the board had to carry home bundles of reports to study.

Finally, Mr. Howell persuaded the board of directors to take up one problem at a time and come to a decision. No procastination – no putting off. The decision might be to ask for additional facts; it might be to do something or do nothing. But a decision was reached on each problem before passing on to the next. Mr. Howell told me that the results were striking and salutary: the docket was cleared. The calendar was clean. No longer was it necessary for each member to carry home a bundle of reports. No longer was there a worried sense of unresolved problems.

A good rule, not only for the board of directors of U.S. Steel, but for you and me.

Good Working Habit No. 4: Learn to Organise, Deputise and Supervise.

Many a businessman is driving himself to a premature grave because he has never learned to delegate responsibility to others, insists on doing everything himself. Result: details and confusion overwhelm him. He is driven by a sense of hurry, worry, anxiety and tension. It is hard to learn to delegate responsibilities. I know. It was hard for me, awfully hard. I also know from experience the disasters that can be caused by delegating authority to the wrong people. But difficult as it is to delegate authority, the executive must do it if he is to avoid worry, tension, and fatigue.

MEMORY:
HOW TO DEVELOP, TRAIN
AND USE IT

William Walker Atkinson

1

MEMORY: ITS IMPORTANCE

It needs very little argument to convince the average thinking person of the great importance of memory, although even then very few begin to realize just how important is the function of the mind that has to do with the retention of mental impressions. The first thought of the average person when he is asked to consider the importance of memory, is its use in the affairs of everyday life, along developed and cultivated lines, as contrasted with the lesser degrees of its development. In short, one generally thinks of memory in its phase of "a good memory" as contrasted with the opposite phase of "a poor memory". But there is a much broader and fuller meaning of the term than that of even this important phase.

It is true that the success of the individual in his everyday business, profession, trade or other occupation depends very materially upon the possession of a good memory. His value in any walk in life depends to a great extent upon the degree of memory he may have developed. His memory of faces, names, facts, events, circumstances and other things concerning his everyday work is the measure of his ability to accomplish his task. And in the social intercourse of men and women, the possession of a retentive memory, well stocked with available facts, renders its possessor a desirable member of society. And in the higher activities of thought, the memory comes as an invaluable aid to the individual in marshalling the bits and sections of knowledge he may have acquired, and passing them in review before his cognitive faculties – thus does the soul review its mental possessions. As Alexander Smith has said: "A man's real possession is his memory; in nothing else is he rich; in nothing else is he poor." Richter has said: "Memory is the only paradise from which we cannot be driven away. Grant but memory to us, and we can lose nothing by death." Lactantius says: "Memory tempers prosperity, mitigates adversity, controls youth, and delights old age."

But even the above phases of memory represent but a small segment of its complete circle. Memory is more than "a good memory" – it is the means whereby we perform the largest share of our mental work. As Bacon has said: "All knowledge is but remembrance." And Emerson: "Memory is a primary and fundamental faculty, without which none other can work: the cement, the bitumen, the matrix in which the other faculties are embedded. Without it all life and thought were an unrelated succession." And Burke: "There is no faculty of the mind which can bring its energy into effect unless the memory be stored with ideas for it to look upon." And Basile: "Memory is the cabinet of imagination, the treasury of reason, the registry of conscience, and the council chamber of thought." Kant pronounced memory to be "the most wonderful of the faculties." Kay, one of the best authorities on the subject has said, regarding it: "Unless the mind possessed the power of treasuring up and recalling its past experiences, no knowledge of any kind could be acquired. If every sensation, thought, or emotion passed entirely from the mind the moment it ceased to be present, then it would be as if it had not been; and it could not be recognized or named, should it happen to return. Such as, one would not only be without knowledge – without experience gathered from the past – but without purpose, aim, or plan regarding the future, for these imply knowledge and require memory. Even voluntary motion, or motion for a purpose, could have no existence without memory, for memory is involved in every purpose. Not only the learning of the scholar, but the inspiration of the poet, the genius of the painter, the heroism of the warrior, all depend upon memory. Nay, even consciousness itself could have no existence without memory for every act of consciousness involves a change from a past state to a present, and did the past state vanish the moment it was past, there could be no consciousness of change. Memory, therefore, may be said to be involved in all conscious existence – a property of every conscious being!"

In the building of character and individuality, memory plays an important part, for upon the strength of the impressions received, and the firmness with which they are retained, depends the fibre of character and individuality. Our experiences are indeed the stepping stones to greater attainments, and at the same time our guides and protectors from danger. If the memory serves us well in this respect we are saved the pain of repeating the mistakes of the past, and may also profit by remembering and thus avoiding the mistakes of others. As Beattie says: "When memory is preternaturally defective, experience and knowledge will be deficient in proportion, and imprudent conduct and absurd opinion are the necessary consequence." Bain says: "A character retaining a feeble hold of bitter experience, or genuine delight, and unable to revive afterwards the impression of the time is in reality the victim of an intellectual weakness under the guise of a moral weakness. To have constantly before us an estimate of the things that affect us, true to the reality, is one precious condition for having our will always stimulated with an accurate reference to our happiness. The thoroughly educated man, in this respect, is he that can carry with him at all times the exact estimate of what he has enjoyed or suffered from every object that has ever affected him, and in case of encounter can present to the enemy as strong a front as if he were under the genuine impression. A full and accurate memory, for pleasure or for pain, is the intellectual basis both of prudence as regards self, and sympathy as regards others."

So, we see that the cultivation of the memory is far more than the cultivation and development of a single mental faculty – it is the cultivation and development of our entire mental being – the development of our *selves*.

To many persons the words memory, recollection, and remembrance, have the same meaning, but there is a great difference in the exact shade of meaning of each term. The student of this book should make the distinction between the terms, for by so doing he will be better able to grasp the various points of advice and instruction herein given. Let us examine these terms.

Locke in his celebrated work, the "Essay Concerning Human Understanding" has clearly stated the difference between the meaning of these several terms. He says: "Memory is the power to revive again in our minds those ideas which after imprinting, have disappeared, or have been laid aside out of sight – when an idea again recurs without the operation of the like object on the external sensory, it is *remembrance*; if it be sought after by the mind, and with pain and endeavor found, and brought again into view, it is *recollection*." Fuller says, commenting on this: "Memory is the power of reproducing in the mind former impressions, or percepts. Remembrance and Recollection are the exercise of that power, the former being involuntary or spontaneous, the latter volitional. We remember because we cannot help it, but we recollect only through positive effort. The act of remembering, taken by itself, is involuntary. In other words, when the mind remembers without having tried to remember, it acts spontaneously. Thus it

133

may be said, in the narrow, contrasted senses of the two terms that we remember by chance, but recollect by intention, and if the endeavor be successful that which is reproduced becomes, by the very effort to bring it forth, more firmly entrenched in the mind than ever."

But the New Psychology makes a little different distinction from that of Locke, as given above. It uses the word memory not only in his sense of "The power to revive, etc.," but also in the sense of the activities of the mind which tend to receive and store away the various impressions of the senses, and the ideas conceived by the mind, to the end that they may be reproduced voluntarily, or involuntarily, thereafter. The distinction between remembrance and recollection, as made by Locke, is adopted as correct by The New Psychology.

It has long been recognized that the memory, in all of its phases, is capable of development, culture, training and guidance through intelligent exercise. Like any other faculty of mind, or physical part, muscle or limb, it may be improved and strengthened. But until recent years, the entire efforts of these memory-developers were directed to the strengthening of that phase of the memory known as "recollection," which, you will remember, Locke defined as an idea or impression "sought after by the mind, and with pain and endeavor found, and brought again into view." The New Psychology goes much further than this. While pointing out the most improved and scientific methods for "re-collecting" the impressions and ideas of the memory, it also instructs the student in the use of the proper methods whereby memory may be stored with clear and distinct impressions which will, thereafter, flow naturally and involuntarily into the field of consciousness when the mind is thinking upon the associated subject or line of thought; and which may also be "re-collected" by a voluntary effort with far less expenditure of energy than under the old methods and systems.

You will see this idea carried out in detail, as we progress with the various stages of the subject, in this work. You will see that the first thing to do is *to find something to remember*; then to impress that thing clearly and distinctly upon the receptive tablets of the memory; then to exercise the remembrance in the direction of bringing out the stored-away facts of the memory; then to acquire the scientific methods of recollecting special items of memory that may be necessary at some special time. This is the natural method in memory cultivation, as opposed to the artificial systems that you will find mentioned in another chapter. It is not only development of the memory, but also development of the mind itself in several of its regions and phases of activity. It is not merely a method of recollecting, but also a method of correct seeing, thinking and remembering. This method recognizes the truth of the verse of the poet, Pope, who said: "Remembrance and reflection how allied! What thin partitions sense from thought divide!"

2

CULTIVATION OF THE MEMORY

This book is written with the fundamental intention and idea of pointing out a rational and workable method whereby memory may be developed, trained and cultivated. Many persons seem to be under the impression that memories are bestowed by nature, in a fixed degree or possibilities, and that little more can be done for them – in short, that memories are born, not made. But the fallacy of any such idea is demonstrated by the investigations and experiments of all the leading authorities, as well as by the results obtained by persons who have developed and cultivated their own memories by individual effort without the assistance of an instructor. But all such improvement, to be real, must be along certain natural lines and in accordance with the well-established laws of psychology, instead of along artificial lines and in defiance of psychological principles. Cultivation of the memory is a far different thing from "trick memory," or feats of mental legerdemain if the term is permissible.

Kay says: "That the memory is capable of indefinite improvement, there can be no manner of doubt; but with regard to the means by which this improvement is to be effected mankind are still greatly in ignorance." Dr. Noah Porter says: "The natural as opposed to the artificial memory depends on the relations of sense and the relations of thought, – the spontaneous memory of the eye and the ear availing itself of the obvious conjunctions of objects which are furnished by space and time, and the rational memory of those higher combinations which the rational faculties super induce upon those lower. The artificial memory proposes to substitute for the natural and necessary relations under which all objects must present and arrange themselves, an entirely new set of relations that are purely arbitrary and mechanical, which excite little or no other interest than that they are to aid us in remembering. It follows that if the mind tasks itself to the special effort of considering objects under these artificial relations, it will give less attention to those which have a direct and legitimate interest for itself." Granville says: "The defects of most methods which have been devised and employed for improving the memory, lies in the fact that while they serve to impress particular subjects on the mind, they do not render the memory, as a whole, ready or attentive." Fuller says: "Surely an art of memory may be made more destructive to natural memory than spectacles are to eyes." These opinions of the best authorities might be multiplied indefinitely – the consensus of the best opinion is decidedly against the artificial systems, and in favour of the natural ones.

Natural systems of memory culture are based upon the fundamental conception so well expressed by Helvetius, several centuries ago, when he said: "The extent of the memory depends, first, on the daily use we make of it; secondly, upon the attention with which we consider the objects we would impress upon it; and, thirdly, upon the order in which we range our ideas." This then is the list of the three essentials in the cultivation of the memory: (1) Use and exercise; review and practice; (2) Attention and Interest; and (3) Intelligent Association.

You will find that we urge, first, last, and all the time, the importance of the use and employment of the memory, in the way of employment, exercise, practice and review work. Like any other mental faculty, or physical function, the memory will increase, strengthen and develop by rational exercise and employment within the bounds of moderation. You develop a muscle by exercise; you train any special faculty of the mind in the same way; and you must pursue the same method in the case of the memory, if you wish to a develop it. Nature's laws are constant, and bear a close analogy to each other. You will also notice the great stress that we lay upon the use of the faculty of attention, accompanied by interest. By attention you acquire the impressions that you file away in your mental record-file of memory. And the degree of attention regulates the depth, clearness and strength of the impression. Without a good record, you cannot expect to obtain a good reproduction of it. A poor phonographic record results in a poor reproduction, and the rule applies in the case of the memory as well. You will also notice that we explain the laws of association, and the principles which govern the subject, as well as the methods whereby the proper associations may be made. Every association that you weld to an idea or an impression, serves as a cross-reference in the index, whereby the thing is found by remembrance or recollection when it is needed. We call your attention to the fact that one's entire education depends for its efficiency upon this law of association. It is a most important feature in the rational cultivation of the memory, while at the same time being the bane of the artificial systems. Natural associations educate, while artificial ones tend to weaken the powers of the mind, if carried to any great length.

There is no Royal Road to Memory. The cultivation of the memory depends upon the practice along certain scientific lines according to well established psychological laws. Those who hope for a sure "short cut" will be disappointed, for none such exists. As Halleck says: "The student ought not to be disappointed to find that memory is no exception to the rule of improvement by proper methodical and long continued exercise. There is no royal road, no short cut, to the improvement of either mind or muscle. But the student who follows the rules which psychology has laid down may know that he is walking in the shortest path, and not wandering aimlessly about. Using these rules, he will advance much faster than those without chart, compass, or pilot. He will find mnemonics of extremely limited use. Improvement comes by orderly steps. Methods that dazzle at first sight never give solid results."

The student is urged to pay attention to what we have to say upon the subjects of attention and association. The cultivation of the attention is a prerequisite for good memory, and deficiency in this respect means deficiency not only in the field of memory but also in the general field of mental work. In all branches of The New Psychology there is found a constant repetition of the injunction to cultivate the faculty of attention and concentration. Halleck says: "Haziness of perception lies at the root of many a bad memory. If perception is definite, the first step has been taken towards insuring a good memory. If the first impression is vivid, its effect upon the brain cells is more lasting. All persons ought to practice their visualizing power. This will react upon perception and make it more definite. Visualizing will also form a brain habit of remembering things pictorially, and hence more exactly."

The subject of association must also receive its proper share of attention, for it is by means of association that the stored away records of the memory may be recovered or re-collected. As Blackie says: "Nothing helps the mind as much as order and classification. Classes are few, individuals many: to know the class well is to know what is most essential in the character of the individual, and what burdens the memory least to retain." And as Halleck says regarding the subject of association by relation:

"Whenever we can discover any relation between facts, it is far easier to remember them. The intelligent law of memory may be summed up in these words: Endeavor to link by some thought relation each new mental acquisition to an old one. Bind new facts to other facts by relations of similarity, cause and effect, whole and part, or by any logical relation, and we shall find that when an idea occurs to us, a host of related ideas will flow into the mind. If we wish to prepare a speech or write an article on any subject, pertinent illustrations will suggest themselves. The person whose memory is merely contiguous will wonder how we think of them."

In your study for the cultivation of the memory, along the lines laid down in this book, you have read the first chapter thereof and have informed yourself thoroughly regarding the importance of the memory to the individual, and what a large part it plays in the entire work of the mind. Now acquaint yourself with the possibilities in the direction of cultivating the memory to a high degree, as evidenced by the instances related of the extreme case of development noted therein. Then study the chapter on memory systems, and realize that the only true method is the natural method, which requires work, patience and practice – then make up your mind that you will follow this plan as far as it will take you. Then acquaint yourself with the secret of memory – the sub-conscious region of the mind, in which the records of memory are kept, stored away and indexed, and in which the little mental office-boys are busily at work. This will give you the key to the method. Then take up the tips on attention, and association, respectively, and acquaint yourself with these important principles. Then study about the phases of memory, and take mental stock of yourself, determining in which phase of memory you are strongest, and in which you need development. Then read the two chapters on training the eye and ear, respectively – you need this instruction. Then read over the several chapters on the training of the special phases of the memory, whether you need them or not – you may find something of importance in them. Then read that which gives you some general advice and parting instruction. Then return to the chapters dealing with the particular phases of memory in which you have decided to develop yourself, studying the details of the instruction carefully until you know every point of it. Then, most important of all – *get to work*. The rest is a matter of practice, practice, practice, and rehearsal. Go back to the chapters from time to time, and refresh your mind regarding the details. Re-read each chapter at intervals. Make the book your own, in every sense of the word, by absorbing its contents.

3

SHARPENING YOUR MEMORY

In this chapter we shall call your attention to certain of the general principles already mentioned in the preceding chapters, for the purpose of further impressing them upon your mind, and in order that you may be able to think of and to consider them independent of the details of the special phases of memory. This chapter may be considered in the nature of a general review of certain fundamental principles mentioned in the body of the work.

POINT I. Give to the thing that you wish to memorize, as great a degree of concentrated attention as possible.

We have explained the reason for this advice in many places in the book. The degree of concentrated attention bestowed upon the object under consideration, determines the strength, clearness and depth of the impression received and stored away in the subconsciousness. The character of these stored away impressions determines the degree of ease in remembrance and recollection.

POINT II. In considering an object to be memorized, endeavor to obtain the impressions through as many faculties and senses as possible.

The reason for this advice should be apparent to you, if you have carefully read the preceding chapters. An impression received through both sound and sight is doubly as strong as one received through but one of these channels. You may remember a name, or word, either by having seen it in writing or print; or else by reason of having heard it; but if you have both seen and heard it you have a double impression, and possess two possible ways of reviving the impression. You are able to remember an orange by reason of having seen it, smelt it, felt it and tasted it, and having heard its name pronounced. Endeavor to know a thing from as many sense impressions as possible—use the eye to assist ear-impressions; and the ear to assist in eye-impressions. See the thing from as many angles as possible.

POINT III. Sense impressions may be strengthened by exercising the particular faculty through which the weak impressions are received.

You will find that either your eye memory is better than your ear memory, or vice versa. The remedy lies in exercising the weaker faculty, so as to bring it up to the standard of the stronger.

The eye and ear training will help you along these lines. The same rule applies to the several phases of memory—develop the weak ones, and the strong ones will take care of themselves. The only way to develop a sense or faculty is to intelligently train, exercise and use it. Use, exercise and practice will work miracles in this direction.

POINT IV. Make your first impression strong and firm enough to serve as a basis for subsequent ones.

Get into the habit of fixing a clear, strong impression of a thing to be considered, from the first. Otherwise you are trying to build up a large structure upon a poor foundation. Each time you revive an impression you deepen it, but if you have only a dim impression to begin with, the deepened impressions will not include details omitted in the first one. It is like taking a good sharp negative of a picture that you intend to enlarge afterward. The details lacking in the small picture will not appear in the enlargement; but those that do appear in the small one, will be enlarged with the picture.

POINT V. Revive your impressions frequently and thus deepen them.

You will know more of a picture by seeing it a few minutes every day for a week, than you would by spending several hours before it at one time. So it is with the memory. By recalling an impression a number of times, you fix it indelibly in your mind in such a way that it may be readily found when needed. Such impressions are like favourite tools which you need every little while—they are not apt to be mislaid as are those which are but seldom used. Use your imagination in "going over" a thing that you wish to remember. If you are studying a thing, you will find that this "going over" in your imagination will help you materially in disclosing the things that you have not remembered about it. By thus recognizing your weak points of memory, you may be able to pick up the missing details when you study the object itself the next time.

POINT VI. Use your memory and place confidence in it.

One of the important things in the cultivation of the memory is the actual use of it. Begin to trust it a little, and then more, and then still more, and it will rise to the occasion. The man who has to tie a string around his finger in order to remember certain things, soon begins to cease to use his memory, and in the end forgets to remember the string, or what it is for. There are many details, of course, with which it is folly to charge the memory, but one should never allow his memory to fall into disuse. If you are in an occupation in which the work is done by mechanical helps, then you should exercise the memory by learning verses, or other things, in order to keep it in active practice. Do not allow your memory to atrophy.

POINT VII. Establish as many associations for an impression, as possible.

If you have studied the preceding chapters, you will recognize the value of this point. Association is memory's method of indexing and cross-indexing. Each association renders it easier to remember or recollect the thing. Each association gives you another string to your mental bow. Endeavor to associate a new bit of knowledge with something already known by, and familiar to you. In this way, to avoid the danger of having the thing isolated and alone in your mind—without a label, or index number and name, connect your object or thought to be remembered with other objects or thoughts, by the association of contiguity in space and time, and by relationship of kind, resemblance or oppositeness. Sometimes the latter is very useful, as in the case of the man who said that "Smith reminds me so much of Brown—he's so different." You will often be able to remember a thing by remembering something else that happened at the same place, or about the same time—these things give you the "loose ends" of recollection whereby you may unwind the ball of memory. In the same way, one is often able to recollect names by slowly running over the alphabet, with a pencil, until the sight of the capital first letter of the name brings the memory of those following it—this, however, only when the name has previously been memorized by sight. In the same way the first few notes of a musical selection will enable you to remember the whole air; or the first words of a sentence, the entire speech or selection following it. In trying to remember a thing which has escaped you,

you will find it helpful to think of something associated with that thing, even remotely. A little practice will enable you to recollect the thing along the lines of the faintest association or clue. Some men are adept memory detectives, following this plan. The "loose end" in memory is all the expert requires. Any associations furnish these loose ends. An interesting and important fact to remember in this connection is that if you have some one thing that tends to escape your memory, you may counteract the trouble by noting the associated things that have previously served to bring it into mind with you. The associated thing once noted, may thereafter be used as a loose end with which to unwind the elusive fact or impression. This idea of association is quite fascinating when you begin to employ it in your memory exercises and work. And you will find many little methods of using it. But always use natural association, and avoid the temptation of endeavoring to tie your memory up with the red-tape of the artificial systems.

POINT VIII. Group your impressions.

This is but a form of association, but is very important. If you can arrange your bits of knowledge and fact into logical groups, you will always be master of your subject. By associating your knowledge with other knowledge along the same general lines, both by resemblances and by opposites, you will be able to find what you need just when you need it. Napoleon Bonaparte had a mind trained along these lines. He said that his memory was like a large case of small drawers and pigeon-holes, in which he filed his information according to its kind. In order to do this he used the methods mentioned in this book of comparing the new thing with the old ones, and then deciding into which group it naturally fitted. This is largely a matter of practice and knack, but it may be acquired by a little thought and care, aided by practice. And it will repay one well for the trouble in acquiring it. The following table will be found useful in classifying objects, ideas, facts, etc., so as to correlate and associate them with other facts of a like kind. The table is to be used in the line of questions addressed to oneself regarding the thing under consideration. You will be delighted at the results, after you have caught the knack of applying it.

QUERY TABLE. Ask yourself the following questions regarding the thing under consideration. It will draw out many bits of information and associated knowledge in your mind:

(1) WHAT?

(5) HOW?

(2) WHENCE?

(6) WHY?

(3) WHERE?

(7) WHITHER?

(4) WHEN?

While the above seven queries are given as a means of acquiring clear impressions and associations, they will also serve as a Magic

Key to Knowledge, if you use them intelligently. If you can answer these questions regarding anything, you will know a great deal about that particular thing. And after you have answered them fully, there will be but little unexpressed knowledge regarding that thing left in your memory. Try them on some one thing—you cannot understand them otherwise, unless you have a very good imagination.

THE SCIENCE OF BEING WELL

Wallace D Wattles

1

THE PRINCIPLE OF HEALTH

In the personal application of the Science of Being Well, as in that of the Science of Getting Rich, certain fundamental truths must be known in the beginning, and accepted without question. Some of these truths we state here: –

The perfectly natural performance of function constitutes health; and the perfectly natural performance of function results from the natural action of the Principle of Life. There is a Principle of Life in the universe; it is the One Living Substance from which all things are made. This Living Substance permeates, penetrates, and fills the interspaces of the universe; it is in and through all things, like a very refined and diffusible ether. All life comes from it; its life is all the life there is.

Man is a form of this Living Substance, and has within him a Principle of Health. (The word Principle is used as meaning source.) The Principle of Health in man, when in full constructive activity, causes all the voluntary functions of his life to be perfectly performed.

It is the Principle of Health in man which really works all healing, no matter what "system" or "remedy" is employed; and this Principle of Health is brought into Constructive Activity by thinking in a Certain Way.

I proceed now to prove this last statement. We all know that cures are wrought by all the different, and often opposite, methods employed in the various branches of the healing art. The allopath, who gives a strong dose of a counter-poison, cures his patient; and the homeopath, who gives a diminutive dose of the poison most similar to that of the disease, also cures it. If allopathy ever cured any given disease, it is certain that homeopathy never cured that disease; and if homeopathy ever cured an ailment, allopathy could not possibly cure that ailment. The two systems are radically opposite in theory and practice; and yet both "cure" most diseases. And even the remedies used by physicians in any one school are not the same. Go with a case of indigestion to half a dozen doctors, and compare their prescriptions; it is more than likely that none of the ingredients of any one of them will be in the others. Must we not conclude that their patients are healed by a Principle of Health within themselves, and not by something in the varying "remedies"?

Not only this, but we find the same ailments cured by the osteopath with manipulations of the spine; by the faith healer with prayer, by the food scientist with bills of fare, by the Christian Scientist with a formulated creed statement, by the mental scientist with affirmation, and by the hygienists with differing plans of living. What conclusion can we come to in the face of all these facts but that there is a Principle of Health which is the same in all people, and which really accomplishes all the cures; and that there is something in all the "systems" which, under favorable conditions, arouses the Principle of Health to action? That is, medicines, manipulations, prayers, bills of fare, affirmations, and hygienic practices cure whenever they cause the Principle of Health to become active; and fail whenever they do not cause it to become active. Does not all this indicate that the results depend upon the way the patient thinks about the remedy, rather than upon the ingredients in the prescription?

There is an old story which furnishes so good an illustration on this point that I will give it here. It is said that in the middle ages, the bones of a saint, kept in one of the monasteries, were working miracles of healing. On certain days a great crowd of the afflicted gathered to touch the relics, and all who did so were healed. On the eve of one of these occasions, some sacrilegious rascal gained access to the case in which the wonder-working relics were kept and stole the bones; and in the morning, with the usual crowd of sufferers waiting at the gates, the fathers found themselves shorn of the source of the miracle-working power. They resolved to keep the matter quiet, hoping that by doing so they might find the thief and recover their treasures; and hastening to the cellar of the convent they dug up the bones of a murderer, who had been buried there many years before. These they placed in the case, intending to make some plausible excuse for the failure of the saint to perform his usual miracles on that day; and then they let in the waiting assemblage of the sick and infirm. To the intense astonishment of those in the secret, the bones of the malefactor proved as efficacious as those of the saint; and the healing went on as before. One of the fathers is said to have left a history of the occurrence, in which he confessed that, in his judgment, the healing power had been in the people themselves all the time, and never in the bones at all.

Whether the story is true or not, the conclusion applies to all the cures wrought by all the systems. The Power that Heals is in the patient himself; and whether it shall become active or not does not depend upon the physical or mental means used, but upon the way the patient thinks about these means. There is a Universal Principle of Life, a great spiritual Healing Power; and there is a Principle of Health in man which is related to this Healing Power. This is dormant or active, according to the way a man thinks. He can always quicken it into activity by thinking in a Certain Way.

Your getting well does not depend upon the adoption of some system, or the finding of some remedy; people with your identical ailments have been healed by all systems and all remedies. It does not depend upon climate; some people are well and others are sick in all climates. It does not depend upon avocation, unless in case of those who work under poisonous conditions; people are well in all trades and professions. Your getting well depends upon your beginning to think – and act – in a certain way.

The way a man thinks about things is determined by what he believes about them. His thoughts are determined by his faith, and the results depend upon his making a personal application of his faith. If a man has faith in the efficacy of a medicine, and is able to apply that faith to himself, that medicine will certainly cause him to be cured; but though his faith be great, he will not be cured unless he applies it to himself. Many sick people have faith for others, but none for themselves. So, if he has faith in a system of diet, and can personally apply that faith, it will cure him; and if he has faith in prayers and affirmations and personally applies his faith, prayers and affirmations will cure him. Faith, personally applied, cures; and no matter how great the faith or how persistent the thought, it will not cure without personal application. The Science of Being Well, then, includes the two fields of thought and action. To be well it is not enough that man should merely think in a certain way; he must apply his thought to himself, and he must express and externalize it in his outward life by acting in the same way that he thinks.

2

THE FOUNDATIONS OF FAITH

Before man can think in the certain way which will cause his diseases to be healed, he must believe in certain truths which are here stated:–

All things are made from one Living Substance, which, in its original state, permeates, penetrates, and fills the interspaces of the universe. While all visible things are made from It, yet this Substance, in its first formless condition is in and through all the visible forms that It has made. Its life is in All, and its intelligence is in All.

This Substance creates by thought, and its method is by taking the form of that which it thinks about. The thought of a form held by this substance causes it to assume that form; the thought of a motion causes it to institute that motion. Forms are created by this substance in moving itself into certain attitudes or positions. When Original Substance wishes to create a given form, it thinks of the motions which will produce that form. When it wishes to create a world, it thinks of the motions, perhaps extending through ages, which will result in its coming into the attitude and form of the world; and these motions are made. When it wishes to create an oak tree, it thinks of the sequences of movement, perhaps extending through ages, which will result in the form of an oak tree; and these motions are made. The particular sequences of motion by which differing forms should be produced were established in the beginning; they are changeless. Certain motions instituted in the Formless Substance will forever produce certain forms.

Man's body is formed from the Original Substance, and is the result of certain motions, which first existed as thoughts of Original Substance. The motions which produce, renew, and repair the body of man are called functions, and these functions are of two classes: voluntary and involuntary. The involuntary functions are under the control of the Principle of Health in man, and are performed in a perfectly healthy manner so long as man thinks in a certain way. The voluntary functions of life are eating, drinking, breathing, and sleeping. These, entirely or in part, are under the direction of man's conscious mind; and he can perform them in a perfectly healthy way if he will. If he does not perform them in a healthy way, he cannot long be well. So we see that if man thinks in a certain way, and eats, drinks, breathes, and sleeps in a corresponding way, he will be well.

The involuntary functions of man's life are under the direct control of the Principle of Health, and so long as man thinks in a perfectly healthy way, these functions are perfectly performed; for the action of the Principle of Health is largely directed by man's conscious thought, affecting his subconscious mind.

Man is a thinking centre, capable of originating thought; and as he does not know everything, he makes mistakes and thinks error. Not knowing everything, he believes things to be true which are not true. Man holds in his thought the idea of diseased and abnormal functioning and conditions, and so perverts the action of the Principle of Health, causing diseased and abnormal functioning and conditions within his own body. In the Original Substance there are held only the thoughts of perfect motion; perfect and healthy function; complete life. God never thinks disease or imperfection. But for countless ages men have held thoughts of disease, abnormality, old age, and death; and the perverted functioning resulting from these thoughts has become a part of the inheritance of the race. Our ancestors have, for many generations, held imperfect ideas concerning human form and functioning; and we begin life with racial sub-conscious impressions of imperfection and disease.

This is not natural, or a part of the plan of nature. The purpose of nature can be nothing else than the perfection of life. This we see from the very nature of life itself. It is the nature of life to continually advance towards more perfect living; advancement is the inevitable result of the very act of living. Increase is always the result of active living; whatever lives must live more and more. The seed, lying in the granary, has life, but it is not living. Put it into the soil and it becomes active, and at once begins to gather to itself from the surrounding substance, and to build a plant form. It will so cause increase that a seed head will be produced containing thirty, sixty, or a hundred seeds, each having as much life as the first.

Life, by living, increases.

Life cannot live without increasing, and the fundamental impulse of life is to live. It is in response to this fundamental impulse that Original Substance works, and creates. God must live; and he cannot live except as he creates and increases. In multiplying forms, He is moving on to live more.

The universe is a great advancing life, and the purpose of nature is the advancement of life towards perfection; towards perfect functioning. The purpose of nature is perfect health.

The purpose of Nature, so far as man is concerned, is that he should be continuously advancing into more life, and progressing toward perfect life; and that he should live the most complete life possible in his present sphere of action.

This must be so, because that which lives in man is seeking more life.

Give a little child a pencil and paper, and he begins to draw crude figures. That which lives in him is trying to express itself in art. Give him a set of blocks, and he will try to build something; That which lives in him is seeking expression in architecture.

Seat him at a piano, and he will try to draw harmony from the keys. That which lives in him is trying to express itself in music. That which lives in man is always seeking to live more; and since man lives most when he is well, the principle of Nature in him can seek only health. The natural state of man is a state of perfect health; and everything in him, and in nature, tends toward health.

Sickness can have no place in the thought of Original Substance, for it is by its own nature continually impelled toward the fullest and most perfect life; therefore, toward health. Man, as he exists in the thought of the Formless Substance, has perfect health. Disease, which is abnormal or perverted function – motion imperfectly made, or made in the direction of imperfect life – has no place in the thought of the Thinking Stuff.

The Supreme Mind never thinks of disease. Disease was not created or ordained by God, or sent forth from him. It is wholly a product of separate consciousness; of the individual thought of man. God, the Formless Substance, does not see disease, think disease, know disease, or recognize disease. Disease is recognized only by the thought of man. God thinks nothing but health.

From all the foregoing, we see that health is *a fact* or truth in the original substance from which we are all formed; and that disease is imperfect functioning, resulting from the imperfect thoughts of men, past and present. If man's thoughts of himself had always been those of perfect health, man could not possibly now be otherwise than perfectly healthy.

Man in perfect health is the thought of Original Substance, and man in imperfect health is the result of his own failure to think perfect health, and to perform the voluntary functions of life in a healthy way. We will here arrange in a syllabus the basic truths of the Science of Being Well:

There is a Thinking Substance from which all things are made, and which, in its original state, permeates, penetrates, and fills the interspaces of the universe. It is the life of All.

The thought of a form in this Substance causes the form; the thought of a motion produces the motion. In relation to man, the thoughts of this Substance are always of perfect functioning and perfect health.

Man is a thinking center, capable of original thought; and his thought has power over his own functioning. By thinking imperfect thoughts he has caused imperfect and perverted functioning; and by performing the voluntary functions of life in a perverted manner, he has assisted in causing disease.

If man will think only thoughts of perfect health, he can cause within himself the functioning of perfect health; all the Power of Life will be exerted to assist him. But this healthy functioning will not continue unless man performs the external, or voluntary, functions of living in a healthy manner.

Man's first step must be to learn how to think perfect health; and his second step to learn how to eat, drink, breathe, and sleep in a perfectly healthy way. If man takes these two steps, he will certainly become well, and remain so.

3

LIFE AND ITS ORGANISMS

The human body is the abiding place of an energy which renews it when worn; which eliminates waste or poisonous matter, and which repairs the body when broken or injured. This energy we call life. Life is not generated or produced within the body; *it produces the body*.

The seed which has been kept in the storehouse for years will grow when planted in the soil; it will produce a plant. But the life in the plant is not generated by its growing; it is the life which makes the plant grow.

The performance of function does not cause life; it is life which causes function to be performed. Life is first; function afterward.

It is life which distinguishes organic from inorganic matter, but it is not produced after the organization of matter.

Life is the principle or force which causes organization; it builds organisms.

It is a principle or force inherent in Original Substance; all life is One.

This Life Principle of the All is the Principle of Health in man, and becomes constructively active whenever man thinks in a certain way. Whoever, therefore, thinks in this Certain Way will surely have perfect health if his external functioning is in conformity with his thought. But the external functioning must conform to the thought; man cannot hope to be well by thinking health, if he eats, drinks, breathes, and sleeps like a sick man.

The universal Life Principle, then, is the Principle of Health in man. It is one with original substance. There is one Original Substance from which all things are made; this substance is alive, and its life is the Principle of Life of the universe. This Substance has created from itself all the forms of organic life by thinking them, or by thinking the motions and functions which produce them.

Original Substance thinks only health, because It knows all truth; there is no truth which is not known in the Formless, which is All, and in all. It not only knows all truth, but it has all power; its vital power is the source of all the energy there is. A conscious life which knows all truth and which has all power cannot go wrong or perform function imperfectly; knowing all, it knows, too much to go wrong, and so the Formless cannot be diseased or think disease.

Man is a form of this original substance, and has a separate consciousness of his own; but his consciousness is limited, and therefore imperfect. By reason of his limited knowledge man can and does think wrongly, and so he causes perverted and imperfect functioning in his own body. Man has not known too much to go wrong. The diseased or imperfect functioning may not instantly result from an imperfect thought, but it is bound to come if the thought becomes habitual. Any thought continuously held by man tends to the establishment of the corresponding condition in his body.

Also, man has failed to learn how to perform the voluntary functions of his life in a healthy way. He does not know when, what, and how to eat; he knows little about breathing, and less about sleep. He does all these things in a wrong way, and under wrong conditions; and this because he has neglected to follow the only sure guide to the knowledge of life. He has tried to live by logic rather than by instinct; he has made living a matter of art, and not of nature. And he has gone wrong.

His only remedy is to begin to go right; and this he can surely do. It is the work of this book to teach the whole truth, so that the man who reads it shall know too much to go wrong.

The thoughts of disease produce the forms of disease. Man must learn to think health; and being Original Substance which takes the form of its thoughts, he will become the form of health and manifest perfect health in all his functioning. The people who were healed by touching the bones of the saint were really healed by thinking in a certain way, and not by any power emanating from the relics. There is no healing power in the bones of dead men, whether they be those of saint or sinner.

The people who were healed by the doses of either the allopath or the homeopath were also really healed by thinking in a certain way; there is no drug which has within itself the power to heal disease.

The people who have been healed by prayers and affirmations were also healed by thinking in a certain way; there is no curative power in strings of words.

All the sick who have been healed, by whatsoever "system," have thought in a certain way; and a little examination will show us what this way is.

The two essentials of the Way are Faith, and a Personal Application of the Faith.

The people who touched the saint's bones had faith; and so great was their faith that in the instant they touched the relics they severed all mental relations with disease, and mentally unified themselves with health.

This change of mind was accompanied by an intense devotional feeling which penetrated to the deepest recesses of their souls, and so aroused the Principle of Health to powerful action. By faith they claimed that they were healed, or appropriated health to themselves; and in full faith they ceased to think of themselves in connection with disease and thought of themselves only in connection with health.

These are the two essentials to thinking in the Certain Way which will make you well: first, claim or appropriate health by faith; and, second, sever all mental relations with disease, and enter into mental relations with health. That which we make ourselves mentally, we become physically; and that with which we unite ourselves mentally, we become unified with physically. If your thought always relates you to disease, then your thought becomes a fixed power to cause disease within you; and if your thought always relates you to health, then your thought becomes a fixed power exerted to keep you well.

In the case of the people who are healed medicines, the result is obtained in the same way. They have, consciously or unconsciously, sufficient faith in the means used to cause them to sever mental relations with disease and enter into mental relations with health. Faith may be unconscious. It is possible for us to have a subconscious or inbred faith in things like medicine, in which we do not believe to any extent objectively; and this subconscious faith may be quite sufficient to quicken the Principle of Health into constructive activity. Many who have little conscious faith are healed in this way; while many others who have great faith in the means are not healed because they do not make the personal application to themselves; their faith is general, but not specific for their own cases.

In the Science of Being Well we have two main points to consider: first, how to think with faith; and, second, how to so apply the thought to ourselves as to quicken the Principle of Health into constructive activity. We begin by learning What to Think.

4

WHAT TO THINK

In order to sever all mental relations with disease, you must enter into mental relations with health, making the process positive not negative; one of assumption, not of rejection. You are to receive or appropriate health rather than to reject and deny disease. Denying disease accomplishes next to nothing; it does little good to cast out the devil and leave the house vacant, for he will presently return with others worse than himself. When you enter into full and constant mental relations with health, you must of necessity cease all relationship with disease. The first step in the Science of Being Well is, then, to enter into complete thought connection with health.

The best way to do this is to form a mental image or picture of yourself as being well, imagining a perfectly strong and healthy body; and to spend sufficient time in contemplating this image to make it your habitual thought of yourself.

This is not so easy as it sounds; it necessitates the taking of considerable time for meditation, and not all persons have the imaging faculty well enough developed to form a distinct mental picture of themselves in a perfect or idealized body. It is much easier to form a mental image of the things one wants to have; for we have seen these things, or their counterparts, and know how they look; we can picture them very easily from memory. But we have never seen ourselves in a perfect body, and a *clear* mental image is hard to form.

It is not necessary or essential, however, to have a clear mental image of yourself as you wish to be; it is only essential to form a conception of perfect health, and to relate yourself to it. This Conception of Health is not a mental picture of a particular thing; it is an understanding of health, and carries with it the idea of perfect functioning in every part and organ.

You may try to picture yourself as perfect in physique; that helps; and you must *think of yourself as doing everything in the manner of a perfectly strong and healthy person.* You can picture yourself as walking down the street with an erect body and a vigorous stride; you can picture yourself as doing your day's work easily and with surplus vigor, never tired or weak; you can picture in your mind how all things would be done by a person full of health and power, and you can make yourself the central figure in the picture, doing things in just that way. Never think of the ways in which weak or sickly people do things; always think of the way strong people do things. Spend your leisure time in thinking about the Strong Way, until you have a good conception of it; and always think of yourself in connection with the Strong Way of Doing Things. That is what I mean by having a Conception of Health.

In order to establish perfect functioning in every part, man does not have to study anatomy or physiology, so that he can form a mental image of each separate organ and address himself to it. He does not have to "treat" his liver, his kidneys, his stomach, or his heart. There is one Principle of Health in man, which has control over all the involuntary functions of his life; and the thought of perfect health, impressed upon this Principle, will reach each part and organ. Man's liver is not controlled by a liver-principle, his stomach by a digestive principle, and so on; the Principle of Health is One.

The less you go into the detailed study of physiology, the better for you. Our knowledge of this science is very imperfect, and leads to imperfect thought. Imperfect thought causes imperfect functioning, which is disease. Let me illustrate: Until quite recently, physiology fixed ten days as the extreme limit of man's endurance without food; it was considered that only in exceptional cases could he survive a longer fast. So the impression became universally disseminated that one who was deprived of food must die in five to ten days; and numbers of people, when cut off from food by shipwreck, accident, or famine, did die within this period. But the performances of Dr. Tanner, the forty-day faster, and the writings of Dr. Dewey and others on the fasting cure, together with the experiments of numberless people who have fasted from forty to sixty days, have shown that man's ability to live without food is vastly greater than had been supposed. Any person, properly educated, can fast from twenty to forty days with little loss in weight, and often with no apparent loss of strength at all. The people who starved to death in ten days or less did so because they believed that death was inevitable; an erroneous physiology had given them a wrong thought about themselves. When a man is deprived of food he will die in from ten to fifty days, according to the way he has been taught; or, in other words, according to the way he thinks about it. So you see that an erroneous physiology can work very mischievous results.

No Science of Being Well can be founded on current physiology; it is not sufficiently exact in its knowledge. With all its pretensions, comparatively little is really known as to the interior workings and processes of the body. It is not known just how food is digested; it is not known just what part food plays, if any, in the generation of force. It is not known exactly what the liver, spleen, and pancreas are for, or what part their secretions play in the chemistry of assimilation. On all these and most other points we theorize, but we do not really know. When man begins to study physiology, he enters the domain of theory and disputation; he comes among conflicting opinions, and he is bound to form mistaken ideas concerning himself. These mistaken ideas lead to the thinking of wrong thoughts, and this leads to perverted functioning and disease. All that the most perfect knowledge of physiology could do for man would be to enable him to think only thoughts of perfect health, and to eat, drink, breathe, and sleep in a perfectly healthy way; and this, as we shall show, he can do without studying physiology at all.

This, for the most part, is true of all hygiene. There are certain fundamental propositions which we should know; and these will be explained in later chapters, but aside from these propositions, ignore physiology and hygiene. They tend to fill your mind with thoughts of imperfect conditions, and these thoughts will produce the imperfect conditions in your own body. You cannot study any "science" which recognizes disease, if you are to think nothing but health.

Drop all investigation as to your present condition, its causes, or possible results, and set yourself to the work of forming a conception of health.

Think about health and the possibilities of health; of the work that may be done and the pleasures that may be enjoyed in a condition of perfect health. Then make this conception your guide in thinking of yourself; refuse to entertain for an instant any thought of yourself which is not in harmony with it. When any idea of disease or imperfect functioning enters your mind, cast it out instantly by calling up a thought which is in harmony with the Conception of Health.

Think of yourself at all times as realizing conception; as being a strong and perfectly healthy personage; and do not harbor a contrary thought.

Know that as you think of yourself in unity with this conception, the Original Substance which permeates and fills the tissues of your body is taking form according to the thought; and know that this Intelligent Substance or mind stuff will cause function to be performed in such a way that your body will be rebuilt with perfectly healthy cells.

The Intelligent Substance, from which all things are made, permeates and penetrates all things; and so it is in and through your body. It moves according to its thoughts; and so if you hold only the thoughts of perfectly healthy function, it will cause the movements of perfectly healthy function within you.

Hold with persistence to the thought of perfect health in relation to yourself; do not permit yourself to think in any other way. Hold this thought with perfect faith that it is the fact, the truth. It is the truth so far as your mental body is concerned. You have a mind-body and a physical body; the mind-body takes form just as you think of yourself, and any thought which you hold continuously is made visible by the transformation of the physical body into its image. Implanting the thought of perfect functioning in the mind-body will, in due time, cause perfect functioning in the physical body.

The transformation of the physical body into the image of the ideal held by the mind-body is not accomplished instantaneously; we cannot transfigure our physical bodies at will. In the creation and recreation of forms, Substance moves along the fixed lines of growth it has established; and the impression upon it of the health thought causes the healthy body to be built cell by cell. Holding only thoughts of perfect health will ultimately cause perfect functioning; and perfect functioning will in due time produce a perfectly healthy body. It may be as well to condense this chapter into a syllabus:–

Your physical body is permeated and fitted with an Intelligent Substance, which forms a body of mind-stuff. This mind-stuff controls the functioning of your physical body. A thought of disease or of imperfect function, impressed upon the mind-stuff, causes disease or imperfect functioning in the physical body. If you are diseased, it is because wrong thoughts have made impressions on this mind-stuff; these may have been either your own thoughts or those of your parents; we begin life with many subconscious impressions, both right and wrong. But the natural tendency of all mind is toward health, and if no thoughts are held in the conscious mind save those of health, all internal functioning will come to be performed in a perfectly healthy manner.

The Power of Nature within you is sufficient to overcome all hereditary impressions, and if you will learn to control your thoughts, so that you shall think only those of health, and if you will perform the voluntary functions of life in a perfectly healthy way, you can certainly be well.

5

SUMMARY OF
THE MENTAL ACTIONS

Let me now summarize the mental actions and attitudes necessary to the practice of the Science of Being Well: first, you believe that there is a Thinking Substance, from which all things are made, and which, in its original state, permeates, penetrates, and fills the interspaces of the universe. This Substance is the Life of All, and is seeking to express more life in all. It is the Principle of Life of the universe, and the Principle of Health in man.

Man is a form of this Substance, and draws his vitality from it; he is a mind-body of original substance, permeating a physical body, and the thoughts of his mind-body control the functioning of his physical body. If man thinks no thoughts save those of perfect health, the functions of his physical body will be performed in a manner of perfect health.

If you would consciously relate yourself to the All-Health, your purpose must be to live fully on every plane of your being. You must want all that there is in life for body, mind, and soul; and this will bring you into harmony with all the life there is. The person who is in conscious and intelligent harmony with All will receive a continuous inflow of vital power from the Supreme Life; and this inflow is prevented by angry, selfish or antagonistic mental attitudes. If you are against any part, you have severed relations with all; you will receive life, but only instinctively and automatically; not intelligently and purposefully. You can see that if you are mentally antagonistic to any part, you cannot be in complete harmony with the Whole; therefore, be reconciled to everybody and everything before you offer worship.

Want for everybody all that you want for yourself.

The reader is recommended to read concerning the Competitive mind and the Creative mind. It is very doubtful whether one who has lost health can completely regain it so long as he remains in the competitive mind.

Being on the Creative or Good-Will plane in mind, the next step is to form a conception of yourself as in perfect health, and to hold no thoughts which are not in full harmony with this conception. Have faith that if you think only thoughts of health, you will establish in your physical body the functioning of health; and use your will to determine that you will think only thoughts of health. Never think of yourself as sick, or as likely to be sick; never think of sickness in connection with yourself at all. And, as far as may be, shut out of your mind all thoughts of sickness in connection with others. Surround yourself as much as possible with the things which suggest the ideas of strength and health.

Have faith in health, and accept health as an actual present fact in your life. Claim health as a blessing bestowed upon you by the Supreme Life, and be deeply grateful at all times. Claim the blessing by faith; know that it is yours, and never admit a contrary thought to your mind.

Use your will-power to withhold your attention from every appearance of disease in yourself and others; do not study disease, think about it, nor speak of it. At all times, when the thought of disease is thrust upon you, move forward into the mental position of prayerful gratitude for your perfect health.

The mental actions necessary to being well may now be summed up in a single sentence: Form a conception of yourself in perfect health, and think only those thoughts which are in harmony with that conception.

That, with faith and gratitude, and the purpose to really live, covers all the requirements. It is not necessary to take mental exercises of any kind, or to do wearying "stunts" in the way of affirmations, and so on. It is not necessary to concentrate the mind on the affected parts; it is far better not to think of any part as affected. It is not necessary to "treat" yourself by auto-suggestion, or to have others treat you in any way whatever. The power that heals is the Principle of Health within you; and to call this Principle into Constructive Action it is only necessary, having harmonized yourself with the All-Mind, to claim by faith the All-Health; and to hold that claim until it is physically manifested in all the functions of your body.

In order to hold this mental attitude of faith, gratitude, and health, however, your external acts must be only those of health. You cannot long hold the internal attitude of a well person if you continue to perform the external acts of a sick person. It is essential not only that your every thought should be a thought of health, but that your every act should be an act of health, performed in a healthy manner. If you will make every thought a thought of health, and every conscious act an act of health, it must infallibly follow that every internal and unconscious function shall come to be healthy; for all the power of life is being continually exerted toward health. We shall next consider how you may make every act an act of health.

6

BREATHIN

The function of breathing is a vital one, and it immediately concerns the continuance of life. We can live many hours without sleeping, and many days without eating or drinking, but only a few minutes without breathing. The act of breathing is involuntary, but the manner of it, and the provision of the proper conditions for its healthy performance, falls within the scope of volition. Man will continue to breathe involuntarily, but he can voluntarily determine what he shall breathe, and how deeply and thoroughly he shall breathe; and he can, of his own volition, keep the physical mechanism in condition for the perfect performance of the function.

It is essential, if you wish to breathe in a perfectly healthy way, that the physical machinery used in the act should be kept in good condition. You must keep your spine moderately straight, and the muscles of your chest must be flexible and free in action. You cannot breathe in the right way if your shoulders are greatly stooped forward and your chest hollow and rigid. Sitting or standing at work in a slightly stooping position tends to produce hollow chest; so does lifting heavy weights – or light weights.

The tendency of work, of almost all kinds, is to pull the shoulders forward, curve the spine, and flatten the chest; and if the chest is greatly flattened, full and deep breathing becomes impossible, and perfect health is out of the question.

Various gymnastic exercises have been devised to counteract the effect of stooping while at work; such as hanging by the hands from a swing or trapeze bar, or sitting on a chair with the feet under some heavy article of furniture and bending backward until the head touches the floor, and so on. All these are good enough in their way, but very few people will follow them long enough and regularly enough to accomplish any real gain in physique. The taking of "health exercises" of any kind is burdensome and unnecessary; there is a more natural, simpler, and much better way.

This better way is to keep yourself straight, and to breathe deeply. Let your mental conception of yourself be that you are a perfectly straight person, and whenever the matter comes to your mind, be sure that you instantly expand your chest, throw back your shoulders, and "straighten up." Whenever you do this, slowly draw in your breath until you fill your lungs to their utmost capacity; "crowd in" all the air you possibly can; and while holding it for an instant in the lungs, throw your shoulders still further back, and stretch your chest; at the same time try to pull your spine forward between the shoulders. Then let the air go easily.

This is the one great exercise for keeping the chest full, flexible, and in good condition. Straighten up; fill your lungs; stretch your chest and straighten your spine, and exhale easily. And this exercise you must repeat, in season and out of season, at all times and in all places, until you form a habit of doing it; you can easily do so. Whenever you step out of doors into the fresh, pure air, breathe. When you are at work, and think of yourself and your position, breathe. When you are in company, and are reminded of the matter, breathe. When you are awake in the night, breathe. No matter where you are or what you are doing, whenever the idea comes to your mind, straighten up and breathe. If you walk to and from your work, take the exercise all the way; it will soon become a delight to you; you will keep it up, not for the sake of health, but as a matter of pleasure.

Do not consider this a "health exercise"; *never take health exercises, or do gymnastics to make you well. To do so is to recognize sickness as a present fact or as a possibility, which is precisely what you must not do.* The people who are always taking exercises for their health are always thinking about being sick. It ought to be a matter of pride with you to keep your spine straight and strong; as much as it is to keep your face clean. Keep your spine straight, and your chest full and flexible for the same reason that you keep your hands clean and your nails manicured; because it is slovenly to do otherwise. Do it without a thought of sickness, present or possible. You must either be crooked and unsightly, or you must be straight; and if you are straight your breathing will take care of itself. You will find the matter of health exercises referred to again in a future chapter.

It is essential, however, that you should breathe air. It appears to be the intention of nature that the lungs should receive air containing its regular percentage of oxygen, and not greatly contaminated by other gases, or by filth of any kind. Do not allow yourself to think that you are compelled to live or work where the air is not fit to breathe. If your house cannot be properly ventilated, move; and if you are employed where the air is bad, get another job; you can, by practicing the methods given in the preceding volume of this series. If no one would consent to work in bad air, employers would speedily see to it that all work rooms were properly ventilated. The worst air is that from which the oxygen has been exhausted by breathing; as that of churches and theaters where crowds of people congregate, and the outlet and supply of air are poor. Next to this is air containing other gases than oxygen and hydrogen – sewer gas, and the effluvium from decaying things. Air that is heavily charged with dust or particles of organic matter may be endured better than any of these. Small particles of organic matter other than food are generally thrown off from the lungs; but gases go into the blood.

I speak advisedly when I say "other than food." Air is largely a food. It is the most thoroughly alive thing we take into the body. Every breath carries in millions of microbes, many of which are assimilated. The odors from earth, grass, tree, flower, plant, and from cooking foods are foods in themselves; they are minute particles of the substances from which they come, and are often so attenuated that they pass directly from the lungs into the blood, and are assimilated without digestion. And the atmosphere is permeated with the One Original Substance, which is life itself. Consciously recognize this whenever you think of your breathing, and think that you are breathing in life; you really are, and conscious recognition helps the process. See to it that you do not breathe air containing poisonous gases, and that you do not rebreathe the air which has been used by yourself or others.

That is all there is to the matter of breathing correctly. Keep your spine straight and your chest flexible, and breathe pure air, recognizing with thankfulness the fact that you breathe in the Eternal Life. That is not difficult; and beyond these things give little thought to your breathing except to thank God that you have learned how to do it perfectly.

6

SLEEP

Vital power is renewed in sleep. Every living thing sleeps; men, animals, reptiles, fish, and insects sleep, and even plants have regular periods of slumber. And this is because it is in sleep that we come into such contact with the Principle of Life in nature that our own lives may be renewed. It is in sleep that the brain of man is recharged with vital energy, and the Principle of Health within him is given new strength. It is of the first importance, then, that we should sleep in a natural, normal, and perfectly healthy manner.

Studying sleep, we note that the breathing is much deeper, and more forcible and rhythmic than in the waking state. Much more air is inspired when asleep than when awake, and this tells us that the Principle of Health requires large quantities of some element in the atmosphere for the process of renewal. If you would surround sleep with natural conditions, then, the first step is to see that you have an unlimited supply of fresh and pure air to breathe. Physicians have found that sleeping in the pure air of out-of-doors is very efficacious in the treatment of pulmonary troubles; and, taken in connection with the Way of Living and Thinking prescribed in this book, you will find that it is just as efficacious in curing every other sort of trouble. Do not take any half-way measures in this matter of securing pure air while you sleep. Ventilate your bedroom thoroughly; so thoroughly that it will be practically the same as sleeping out of doors. Have a door or window open wide; have one open on each side of the room, if possible. If you cannot have a good draught of air across the room, pull the head of your bed close to the open window, so that the air from without may come fully into your face. No matter how cold or unpleasant the weather, have a window open, and open wide; and try to get a circulation of pure air through the room. Pile on the bedclothes, if necessary, to keep you warm; but have an unlimited supply of fresh air from out of doors. This is the first great requisite for healthy sleep.

The brain and nerve centers cannot be thoroughly vitalized if you sleep in "dead" or stagnant air; you must have the living atmosphere, vital with nature's Principle of Life. I repeat, do not make any compromise in this matter; ventilate your sleeping room completely, and see that there is a circulation of outdoor air through it while you sleep. You are not sleeping in a perfectly healthy way if you shut the doors and windows of your sleeping room, whether in winter or summer. Have fresh air. If you are where there is no fresh air, move. If your bedroom cannot be ventilated, get into another house.

Next in importance is the mental attitude in which you go to sleep. It is well to sleep intelligently, purposefully, knowing what you do it for. Lie down thinking that sleep is an infallible vitalizer, and go to sleep with a confident faith that your strength is to be renewed; that you will awake full of vitality and health. Put purpose into your sleep as you do into your eating; give the matter your attention for a few minutes, as you go to rest. Do not seek your couch with a discouraged or depressed feeling; go there joyously, to be made whole. Do not forget the exercise of gratitude in going to sleep; before you close your eyes, give thanks to god for having shown you the way to perfect health, and go to sleep with this grateful thought uppermost in your mind. A bedtime prayer of thanksgiving is a mighty good thing; it puts the Principle of Health within you into communication with its source, from which it is to receive new power while you are in the silence of unconsciousness.

You may see that the requirements for perfectly healthy sleep are not difficult. First, to see that you breathe pure air from out of doors while you sleep; and, second, to put the Within into touch with the Living Substance by a few minutes of grateful meditation as you go to bed. Observe these requirements, go to sleep in a thankful and confident frame of mind, and all will be well. If you have insomnia, do not let it worry you. While you lie awake, form your conception of health; meditate with thankfulness on the abundant life which is yours, breathe, and feel perfectly confident that you will sleep in due time; and you will. Insomnia, like every other ailment, must give way before the Principle of Health aroused to full constructive activity by the course of thought and action herein described.

The reader will now comprehend that it is not at all burdensome or disagreeable to perform the voluntary functions of life in a perfectly healthy way. The perfectly healthy way is the easiest, simplest, most natural, and most pleasant way. The cultivation of health is not a work of art, difficulty, or strenuous labor. You have only to lay aside artificial observances of every kind, and eat, drink, breathe, and sleep in the most natural and delightful way; and if you do this, thinking health and only health, you will certainly be well.

Recommended Reading

Are you a dreamer? Is shortage of money stopping you from realising your dreams?

Do you wish to master the art of creating wealth? Then, your search is over!

Power of the Master Mind is a treasure trove of knowledge and insights by the most legendary finance gurus and bestselling authors of all times.

Full of effective financial planning hacks and advices, it will give you a new perspective on creating wealth and paving the way for success!

Pick this book up to learn:

- Helpful strategies on financial planning.
- How highly successful and rich people manage their finances.
- How to make more money and thrive professionally and personally.
- How to change your life and make it better.